D0260491

Servant Leadership for Slow Learners

By J. David Lundy

Authentic
LIFESTYLE

Copyright © 2002 J. David Lundy

First published in 2002 by Authentic Lifestyle
Reprinted 2002

08 07 06 05 04 03 02   8 7 6 5 4 3 2

Authentic Lifestyle is an imprint of Authentic Media,
PO Box 300, Carlisle, Cumbria, CA3 0QS, UK
and PO Box 1047, Waynesboro, GA 30830-2047, USA
www.paternoster-publishing.com

The right of J. David Lundy to be identified as the
Author of this Work has been asserted by him in
accordance with the Copyright, Designs and
Patents Act 1988

*All rights reserved. No part of this publication may be
reproduced, stored in a retrieval system, or transmitted in any
form or by any means, electronic, mechanical, photocopying,
recording or otherwise, without the prior permission of the
publisher or a licence permitting restricted copying.
In the UK such licences are issued by the
Copyright Licensing Agency,
90 Tottenham Court Road, London W1P 9HE.*

British Library Cataloguing in Publication Data
A catalogue record for this book is available from the
British Library

ISBN 1-85078-442-6

Cover Design by Campsie
Typeset by Textype Typesetters, Cambridge
Printed in Great Britain by Cox & Wyman Ltd, Reading, Berkshire

Contents

Foreword   v
Introduction   vii

1 The styles of leadership and what *'tys'* them
   together   1
2 Situational leadership is more than a secular
   buzzword   22
3 Accessibility: Please walk on the grass   42
4 Affability: It's a team sport   61
5 Vulnerability: Leading from a position of
   weakness   88
6 Vitality: Leading from the Source that is higher
   than I   115
7 Teachability: You can always learn something
   new   155
8 Impartiality: Not being impressed by power   178
9 Identifiability: Being sensitive to the cultural
   context   198
10 Stickability: Finishing well, like the Master   211

Conclusion   230
Bibliography   233

Foreword

David Lundy is a close friend and someone I have had the privilege of working with for some decades.

His years of on-the-field experience help make this book what it is. Here is a book from someone who can walk the talk.

Those of us who believe God's Word and believe in world mission need to read this unique book and face head-on the implications. We can learn so much from these pages about being more effective and biblical in our missions and kingdom pursuits.

I believe his emphasis on servant leadership is especially important. I'm concerned that even major church leaders seem to be so ignorant of the true global missions situation and the special challenges facing all of us.

I hope many will be proactive in reading this key book and getting it into the hands of others around the globe.

George Verwer

Introduction

I grew up in an age when *Coles Notes* burst onto the scene. For those too lazy or uncultured to read completely William Shakespeare's *Hamlet* for their English literature exam, *Coles Notes* afforded a quick fix. These notes served as a kind of comic book synopsis of the classic. More recently, another kind of incipient illiteracy has surfaced. This illiteracy is associated with the computer. Whether it is through trying to follow the 'Help' tutorials on the computer itself, or fathoming hard copy manual instructions, millions of people have struggled with varying degrees of frustration in seeking to overcome their difficulty in understanding how to use the computer. To help these newcomers to modern technology mask the embarrassment of finding these helps to be anything but user-friendly (except perhaps for the computer geeks who wrote them), someone designed a best-selling series of instruction manuals called *Computers For Dummies* or *WordPerfect For Dummies*, or whatever. The *For Dummies* series has become a whole growth industry!

With this type of reader in mind, I approach in this book the whole subject of servant leadership. If we leaders – or aspiring leaders – only had to study the secular models of management and leadership, then the art of leadership development might not be so mysterious. How relatively easy by comparison it can be as a leader to walk your staff through the exercise of quantifying things like a vision or a mission statement, or developing objectives and goals out of a corporate purpose. But the Bible presents a theory of leadership which is inimical to the world's definition of it, which cannot so easily be pinned down, let alone expressed practically. That style is best captured by the term 'servant leadership'. Such leadership cannot be characterized by worldly top-down thinking, situational ethics, and 'how-to' reductionism. About this modern management style, Longenecker aptly summarizes it with these words: 'The management profession has fostered the idea that one is qualified to lead after learning how, after mastering the processes and meeting performances'.[1] But the biblical approach to leadership seems to emphasize the character of the leader and the importance of his or her working relationships. People orientation sublimates task orientation. It is the style of leadership demonstrated and proclaimed by the Lord Jesus Christ himself. The clearest statement of his theology of leadership comes in Mark 10 in the context of the incident where James and John were vying over who was to have the most status in heaven. Jesus used the occasion – as he so often did – to do a little kingdom teaching: 'You know that those who are regarded as rulers of the Gentiles lord it over them, and their high officials exercise authority over them. Not so with you. Instead, whoever wants to become great among you must be your servant, and whoever wants to be first must be slave of all. For even the Son of Man did not come to be served, but to serve,

---

[1] Harold L. Longenecker, *Growing Leaders by Design: How to Use Biblical Principles for Leadership Development* (Grand Rapids, MI: Kregel Books, 1995), 18.

and to give his life as a ransom for many' (Mark 10: 43–45).[2]

Given these words, any Christian leader must come to grips with what servant leadership means. The trouble is – if my experience is any guide – we don't get it. There are so many different ideas out there about leadership that we are at a loss to know where, as Christians, we ought to put our feet down when it comes to practising a form of leadership that is consistent with the fundamental model Jesus left us.

In actual fact, the idea of *servanthood* has a well-established New Testament track record. The idea of servanthood takes several forms, and while I do not see the necessity of doing an exhaustive word study of these various terms for the purposes of this book, it would be helpful to make quick reference to them here just to underscore the centrality of this concept to our understanding of the formation of genuinely Christian leadership. The most frequent word translated into English in the NT as *servant* is *diakonos*, used about a hundred times in the NT. In 1 Timothy 3:8,12 and Romans 16:1, for example, it refers to a church ministry position translated as *deacon*. As early as Acts 6:3–5, deacons are organized in the local church, and their role is one of practical service (there, waiting on tables and administratively caring for the church's widows). However, the term also carries with it a wider sense of service, whether in the context of the church (as in Eph. 4:12), as servants of Christ (John 12:26), or to humankind (Mk. 10:43).[3]

Other similar terms include *oiketes* meaning *household servant*, found four times in the NT (Lk. 16:13; Acts 10:7;

---

[2] Unless otherwise indicated, the *New International Version* will be the version quoted in the text.

[3] For an excellent coverage of these different terms for *servant* see John Stott, *The Preacher's Portrait* (Grand Rapids, MI: W.B. Eerdman's, 1972), 103 ff.

Rom. 14:4; 1 Pet. 2:18). Incidentally, our word *domestic* is from the Latin equivalent of *oiketes*, which is *domesticus*, of course referring to a domestic servant. Then there is *doulos*, most powerfully used in the NT with reference to Christ (Phil. 2:7). A *doulos* servant is a bond-slave and hence a servant without any rights (cf. Ex. 21:2–6). Finally there is *huperetes* (John 18:36 being one of four places this term is used in the NT), which originally meant one who rowed in the lower and more demanding level of oarsmen in a ship and hence came to mean *subordinate*. Whichever word you find in the NT with respect to servant leadership, you cannot come away with the sense that it is conceived of as an exalted position. The pyramid of power paradigm seems to have been inverted somehow by Jesus and his followers. Top-down leadership is not 'on'. Power is exercised by servant leaders but they seem to do so from a position or attitude of weakness (for an example of this see Paul talking about himself in 2 Cor. 4:7–12).

To further complicate our confusion as to what servant leadership entails, those of us who seem to have been gifted 'by birth' for leadership (let alone spiritually gifted) find that our style gravitates toward pro-activity, dominance, persuasiveness – the sort of qualities that seem to cut against the grain of biblical values associated with serving others. But we cannot dismiss a serving style of leadership out of hand because evidently Jesus was both a leader (master) and a servant.[4] Nevertheless, as we shall see, there is a big difference between authoritative leadership (which Jesus exhibited) and authoritarian leadership (from which he disassociated himself).[5]

---

[4] Ibid., 133.
[5] Ibid., 80.

If you are like me in your leadership experiences, you have learned the hard way. I have been a slow learner (a dummy) when it comes to servant leadership. Through the providence (or longsuffering patience) of God, I have had the unique opportunity to serve as a leader in three different spheres of Christian ministry. Those have been first of all as a frontline, grass roots missionary, from 1972 to 1978, and then again (part-time) from 1995 to 1999; also as a missions' executive leader, from 1979 to 1994; and finally, as a pastor, from 1995 to the present. Each new role has enabled me to learn new facets of leadership, and more specifically for this study, new dimensions of servanthood. What has brought convergence in my thinking about servant leadership, apart from the varied contexts within which I have had to act as a leader, is that during the nineties I had the good fortune to teach in an MA in Leadership and Management programme in India. Preparation for teaching nationals in India on the subject of leadership widened my exposure to the literature on leadership, both secular and Christian. Prior to that, working on my Doctor of Ministry degree introduced me to literature in the field of practical theology which informed my understanding of pastoral leadership.

It is my conclusion, through reflection on my own habits and pitfalls in leadership, through observation of others in leadership, through my varied experiences of leadership, through my own spiritual odyssey, and through my formal education, that there is much about servant leadership that could be explained better to the novice and the experienced leader. Our fallen natures, poor examples, and worldly views of leadership conspire to keep us in the dark about what Jesus meant when he said that 'if anyone wants to be first [a leader], he must be the very last, and the servant of all' (Mark 9:35). It is for such people who are slow learners and mystified about how to manage others in a Christian way that this book about servant leadership is written. The material has been written with several different types of leaders (or aspiring leaders) in mind – parachurch executives, pastors, lay leaders in churches, and field missionaries with influential roles. Whether you are a theoretician or practitioner of leadership, this book is for you. An extensive bibliography provides opportunity for further research whereas the popular, anecdotal writing style hopefully will attract the average lay person inquisitive about leadership, or aspiring to such a role, to read what is presented.

Whether by design or by accident, I realize now that I have learned some invaluable lessons about what constitutes servant leadership by observing my son, Mark, struggle to face the real world of adulthood while dogged by a learning disability. Somehow when we were praying for the birth of our son, as it turned out, our only child, in India, Linda and I felt led to pray that God would make him a servant of others. We then called him John Mark, after the biblical character who was finally complimented by the apostle Paul as being 'helpful to me in my ministry' (2 Tim. 4:11).

When Mark was about seven years old he had ear surgery performed on him to resolve his chronic ear infections. Unfortunately his heart stopped beating on the operating table for five minutes. Although he recovered well from the surgery, we did not know until many months later that Mark had been forever changed. Oxygen deprivation must have crossed his neurological wiring to the point where he was subsequently unable to easily process things written on the school blackboard so as to transpose them to his notebook. Being quite intelligent, he disguised his disability for some time, but we began to see that his grades had dropped off and that he was getting into trouble with his teachers. The only thing we had noticed until this point was that he seemed to have a shorter attention span than usual. In fact though, inside, Mark knew that he was different from the way he had been before, that something was wrong, and he was ashamed to ask his parents for help. He was seeing words backwards now, for instance, or his eyes would leap over sentences. All this was difficult for a little boy to process.

The teachers labelled him as lazy. At first we dealt with it as a character issue and tried to get Mark to work harder. Finally we discerned that it was more than that and so we took him to a clinical child psychologist. There we learned that Mark had an attention deficit disorder (ADD). However, the schools at that time did not recognize ADD as a genuine disability. Consequently all through Mark's formal learning years he fought an uphill battle to be accepted and to succeed by normal standards.

Nevertheless, he has done remarkably well and is presently working as a counsellor with developmentally disabled adults, as a vocation. Although Linda and I realized from the beginning of his interest in working with society's disadvantaged people that he would not have had the empathy and patience to work with such people if it were not for what he had suffered through, it has only been recently that it has struck me that 'fate' may very well have required Mark to go through this near death experience to enable the Lord to answer our prayers that our son become a servant of others. If our analysis is correct, then think of how close it must be to God's heart that his people learn this lesson of becoming others' servants. Perhaps this gentleness and consideration of the weak and disenfranchised lies at the heart of Scriptures like Psalm 68:5–6 where we read: 'A father of the fatherless and a judge for the widows, is God in his holy habitation. God makes a home for the lonely; he leads out the prisoners into prosperity' (NASB).

A word of warning. Chapters One and Two are highly theoretical. If you want to get to the practical applications right away, skip those two and start with Chapter Three. A word of thanks too. My wife, Linda, has graciously and carefully proofread two drafts of my manuscript as well as offered me constructive advice along the way. Her help signifies all that I mean when I talk about the value of ministering through teams.

Finally, I should like to say that I do not write this book pretending to be an expert, but as a fellow learner. There is much about servant leadership that I still must master. Even what I have learned I must consciously and constantly reactivate since self-denial, the way of the cross, is never easy: but it is the key to unleashing the inherent leadership qualities put to work in the act of effective leading. John Stott assesses this paradox well when he articulates: 'True self-denial (the denial of our false, fallen self) is not the road to self-destruction but the road to self-discovery'.[6] As I continue to trek in the footsteps of the Master, I am hopeful that even this slow learner will make further progress in servant leadership.

---

[6] John Stott, *The Cross of Christ* (Downer's Grove, IL: InterVarsity Press, 1986), 282.

1

The styles of leadership and what 'tys' them together

If there ever were any aspect of Christianity that could be considered counter-cultural, surely it would be leadership. One of the classic books on leadership from a Christian perspective, *Spiritual Leadership*, written by J. Oswald Sanders, captures this distinctiveness about Christian leadership: 'Worldly conceptions of greatness and leadership cannot be carried over into His spiritual kingdom. In that kingdom there is a complete reversal of earth's values ... Not the number of one's servants but the number of whom one serves, is the heavenly criterion of greatness and the real preparation for leadership.'[7]

I don't know about you, but as a young Christian reading that text, it appeared to me to lead to more questions than it answered. It seemed like I had always been a leader, and my practice of leadership had never put me in subservience to those who were following me. Being the eldest of eight children put me in the driver's seat among my siblings before I was knee high to a grasshopper. Leadership seemed to dog my heels wherever I went. I was captain of a school baseball team. The

---

[7] J. Oswald Sanders, *Spiritual Leadership* (Chicago, IL: Moody Press, 1967), 13.

president of the high school concert band. The head of our young people's group at church. To me leadership seemed to be all about the exercise of power, dazzling people with charisma, and being in the limelight.

Looking back, I realize that I did not in the least way lead in the biblical sense of servanthood in those early years. Even after yielding my life to Christ at the age of twenty-one, my first instinct in leadership roles was to dismiss any application of the concept of servanthood, or its stereotypes at least, to my ministry. Did it mean I had to lead out of a sense of weakness? Was there one biblical style of leadership? Was that style marked by kindly acts like opening doors for others and letting them go through first? Did it mean being a kind of referee where everyone had a say and the leader's job was just to steer the discussion? If leadership came so naturally to me, did I now have to unlearn something, or as a result, be disqualified from leadership? For that matter, did this mean that leaders are made and not born? And what about spiritual gifting in relation to leadership?

These are questions that we will consider in this book. The thesis developed here is that servant leadership has more to do with our response to different contexts within which we must exercise leadership than it does to basic styles of leadership. In other words, all different sorts of servant leaders are needed. It will be maintained that while some styles may be more suited to effective leadership than others, all styles of relating to others can be adapted so as to produce outstanding leadership. The leadership style you are born with does not have to be thrown out the window in order for you to exercise leadership biblically. We shall see that certain choices we inevitably face as leaders come our way that result in us bearing crosses that others in the same position might refuse to shoulder – and thus disqualify themselves as servant leaders even though otherwise their natural aptitude might be well-suited to the exercise of leadership. For example, a leader motivated to serve and develop others will delegate responsibility to someone else when it would be easier and more efficient to do that task him or herself. But the leader knows that empowerment of others is crucial to effective long-term leadership and so followers must be given the opportunity to make mistakes. Without the freedom to learn from mistakes, growth will be difficult. The leader may not look so good when results are tallied up, but larger issues are at stake, which the servant leader recognizes. So a leader can be born but also must be made! Natural giftedness as a leader is acceptable – as long as it is brought under the control of the Holy Spirit.

Regardless of the style of leadership exercised – and we shall shortly argue that there are four basic styles of leadership – it has been my observation that certain principles of functioning will be manifested. To help with remembering these traits of servant leadership, which cut across all styles and leadership contexts, I have found that the words describing them end with the letters *TY*. These universal traits which tie (*ty*) together the practice of servant leadership are accessibility, affability, vulnerability, vitality, teachability, impartiality, identifiability, and stickability. Each of these traits will be explained and put under the microscope in future chapters. If you are a missionary, you will find these qualities, it will be contended. If you are a missionary executive, the same qualities will be found. If you are a pastor, you will get a sense of *déjà vu* when it comes to exhibiting these traits. Similarly, if you are a lay leader in your church, these are the characteristics that will distinguish you as a servant leader. Whatever the sphere of service, servant leadership will be expressed in similar ways, even if in the one situation an assertive, directive style of leadership is called for and in another context a consensus-building style is appropriate. Since these principles of servanthood must often consciously be implemented, for they are not always naturally and unconsciously expressed, it could be argued that they involve self-denial. They involve carrying our cross and thus represent the sacrificial love which is at the heart of Christ-likeness and imitation. Gary Corwin has understood this self-denial at the heart of servant leadership when he articulates his point of view about it as follows.

> Over the years I have developed a thesis. It goes something like this. You can only exercise and sustain personal leadership to the extent that you can bear pain. If you can only bear your own pain, you can't really lead. If you can bear and respond only to the pain of your family, your family represents the full scope of your leadership potential. If, however, by God's grace you can recognize and bear the pain of those around you, the breadth of your leadership potential is limited only by the scope of your burden and capacity.[8]

What are these crosses of leadership we must bear? Crosses like learning to delegate, as was just mentioned, when it might be easier to do the job ourselves. Crosses like being able to learn from criticism without becoming defensive. Crosses like not allowing the busyness of leadership to keep you from personal spiritual formation and the pursuit of excellence, that you might feed well the sheep which are under your care. Crosses like

---

[8] Gary Corwin, 'Leadership as Pain-Bearing', *Evangelical Missions Quarterly* (January 1998), 17.

learning to focus on people and results, not only results. Crosses like being accessible and accountable to your colleagues, instead of leading in isolation and with the perks of power. Crosses like being a good listener when you want to 'just do it'. Crosses like admitting your mistakes instead of always posturing strength and invincibility.

Each chapter, then, from the third one onwards, puts a practical spin on servanthood, and insists that these traits of serving our followers ought to be expressed, no matter what our natural leadership style is. If what I contend can be demonstrated to be true, and can be practised no matter what our intrinsic leadership style is, then it is incumbent on us as leaders to adjust our style to suit the situation we work in and the people we work with. That argument I will be seeking to address in the next chapter, and to show how it corresponds with much current secular thinking on the subject. But here we focus on building a case for there being four basic leadership styles. Styles we are born with. Styles that arise out of our conditioning to some extent too, but which are so much a part of us, whether as a result of nature or nurture, that we instinctively and unconsciously slip into this style when we are in the throes of decision making or acting under pressure.

Nature and nurture in leadership styles

Commenting on the role of nature and nurture in determining our style of leadership, Bruce Jones in *Ministerial Leadership in a Managerial World*, says this: 'Some class leadership style as the simple extension of personality . . . Even in early childhood, dominant personality characteristics can be demonstrated . . . Some would attribute these characteristics to child development in the home.

Some psychologists believe that a one-to-one response to role models takes place, so that authoritarian parents tend to breed authoritarian children, and permissive parents breed more permissive children.'[9] Other factors in shaping a predisposition to behave in certain ways in decision making with others (the major function of a leader, we might argue[10]) include cultural, ethical, and theological ones.[11] Authoritarian parents may produce authoritarian children, for instance. Some cultures prefer permissive leaders who are very relational, others authoritarian father figures, and yet others consensus builders.[12] In studying over ten thousand executives and managers for leadership style, Alan Rowe and Richard Mason have come to much the same conclusion, namely, that 'there is something programmed within us, deep within the recesses of our minds, that causes us to view the world in different ways and to react accordingly [and] . . . that there are certain discernible patterns of style that occur over and over again in the general population [and that] . . . it is the consistency of pattern that helps us understand style.'[13] Whatever the source of our 'natural' leadership style, we will seek to convincingly demonstrate that, as

[9] Bruce W. Jones, *Ministerial Leadership in a Managerial World* (Wheaton, IL: Tyndale House, 1988), 98.

[10] Peter F. Drucker makes a case for decision making ability being the key function of the leader in *The Effective Executive* (New York: HarperCollins, 1985).

[11] Bruce Jones, *Ministerial Leadership*, 99.

[12] A growing body of literature addresses the issue of cultural influences in leadership style, which are cited in my book, *We Are the World: Globalisation and the Changing Face of Missions* (Carlisle, UK: OM Publishing, 1999), 88–90.

[13] Alan Rowe and Richard Mason, *Managing With Style: A Guide to Understanding, Assessing, and Improving Decision Making* (San Francisco: Jossey-Bass, 1989), 19.

cross-bearing disciples of Christ, we must not be averse as leaders to consciously making adjustments in the way we operate, or to learning new habits and skills, in order to better serve those who count on us for inspiration and direction. Such is the stuff of which servant leadership is born.

If what I say is true, it deflates much of the current teaching on spiritual gifts, because to intentionally make adjustments in the way we minister, instead of just going with the flow – something that we are told we can expect to happen if we are functioning out of our strengths/ gifting in the power of the Spirit – enables us to minister in a wider range of contexts instead of narrow-niching in the name of 'gifting stewardship'. Understanding how servanthood works across the board should ultimately free us to be ourselves much of the time, paradoxically, by allowing for greater flexibility in how we go about expressing our leadership, and releasing us from the false guilt that thinks that 'my style of leadership cannot be used in the church because it does not fit in with the servanthood model in Scripture'. Well, let us dig in then to examining the literature, and reflecting on some anecdotal observations about styles of leadership.

Left brain versus right brain

At the risk of being over-simplistic and recognizing that the jury is still out on how well we can demarcate different behavioural functions with different brain hemispheres, nonetheless it is generally accepted wisdom that every individual has the left or right hemisphere of their brain predominating in the way they think, make decisions, and behave.[14] Since the four styles presented

---

[14] Ibid., 153–5, 57–67.

here assume a theory of a bicameral neurological basis of decision making, a word about this understanding of human behaviour is in order at the outset.

By left brain we mean, in lay terms, that logical deductive processing is predominating in the choosing of a course of action. In contrast, right brain activity is understood as perceiving and deciding on the basis of relational, spatial, and inductive criteria.[15] In describing how people possess an innate or learned ability to operate more out of the left side of their brain as opposed to the right, or vice versa, Rowe and Mason make this comment: 'Some people have a tendency to focus more on the objective aspects of their environment, which we have called the task or technical orientation [left brain], while others have a tendency to deal more with the subjective aspects of their environment, which we have called the people, social, or organizational orientation [right brain].'[16] This then might explain the tremendous contrasts we see in Scripture between the disciples Peter (surely left brain dominated) and John (right brain oriented). Or between Barnabas (right brain – 'the son of encouragement') and the one whom he discipled and who quickly overshadowed him, Paul (both left and right brain, but perhaps more left).

Contrasting left and right brain functions more popularly, Stephen Covey, through his management seminars and books, would describe the differences this way:

- The left side deals with words, the right with pictures
- The left with parts and specifics, the right with wholes and relationships
- The left with analysis, the right with synthesis

---

[15] Ibid., 57.
[16] Ibid., 58.

- The left with sequences, the right with wholes
- The left is time-bound, the right is time-free[17]

Now here's the trick. Rowe and Mason insist – and seem to be able to demonstrate the validity of their findings empirically – that while an individual's external circumstances may change (e.g. he or she may change jobs and so need to call upon different leadership skills, as in moving from managing a department of accountants in a life insurance firm to being given an executive role as vice president of the actuarial division), that person seldom changes his or her fundamental decision making (leadership) style.[18] Furthermore, Rowe and Mason's findings show that gender or age has only a minor effect on decision making style.

Variations of the styles

While it will be argued here that there are four basic styles of decision making (that is, a way to look at leadership behaviour), it is also important to stress that we are 'fearfully and wonderfully made' (Psalm 139:14). That is to say, there are combinations of styles that stamp us in distinctive ways, so as to make us the unique individuals that we are. Rowe and Mason for example provide evidence for there being 156 permutations of styles.[19] For instance, I have a conceptual style *predominating* but have directive and analytical styles as *backup* ones. Incidentally, the conceptual-directive combination has been shown to

---

[17] Stephen Covey, *Principle-Centered Leadership* (New York: Fireside, 1991), 246–98.

[18] Alan Rowe and Richard Mason, *Managing With Style*, 64.

[19] Ibid., 35.

produce ideal executives.[20] By *dominant* these management consultants and researchers mean that, through the testing of their Decision Style Inventory (DSI), they are able to determine that individuals with this style propensity 'will use this style frequently'. On the other hand, those who have a particular style as *backup* will use it only 'when the occasion demand[s]'. There are also a *least preferred* style (which is seldom used) and a *very dominant* style (which is used in almost every situation).[21]

Complexity among leader types is supported by other behavioural theories which, at the same time, are basically categorizing leadership styles through four grids, which are consistent with what we say below. For instance Myers-Briggs is a widely used personality measurement both with secular and Christian organizations. The testing done by the Myers-Briggs method (MBTI) assumes that there are orderly reasons for personality differences, and that the way people develop their leadership is determined paramountly by these in-born preferences. The MBTI takes Carl Jung's theory as a conceptual framework and considers personality through four dimensions, each of which can be combined with one of the other dimensions as a strength in an individual. In other words, its four styles really expand to 16 styles.[22] And if you want to get more precise or technical, the reality is that those tested manifest even other combinations of these 16 basic style groupings.

Nevertheless, the basic four dimensions are readily observable in people and measure quite different propensities of behaviour or ways of thinking: (1) perceiving through direct observation versus intuition; (2) ways of judging by facts or feelings; (3) ways of

---

[20] Ibid., 171.

[21] Ibid., 38–43.

[22] Cited in Bruce Jones, *Ministerial Leadership*, 107.

responding extrovertedly or introvertedly; and (4) ways of orientation to reality by judgment or perception. Furthermore, in comparing MBTI findings with those of Rowe and Mason's DSI, there appears to be a remarkable correspondence. In other words, the DSI styles which will be described below as being *directive* and *analytical* (left brain styles), or *conceptual* and *behavioural* (right brain styles) could also be classified like the MBTI styles of *ST (sensing/thinking)*, *NT (intuiting/thinking)*, *SF (sensing/feeling)* and *NF (intuiting/feeling)*, respectively.[23]

All that is a long way of saying that in spite of there being complexity when determining distinct or precise styles of leadership in different people, there are actually only four basic styles. Let us then look at the four fundamentally different styles and how they impact how we lead. As we do so, in this chapter, we are concerned with the descriptive side of leadership as opposed to the diagnostic side of leadership. This latter perspective will be dealt with in the next chapter.

Autocratic-directive style

The literature I have been exposed to on leadership styles (Christian and secular) propose what can be boiled down to four basic styles, although there will need to be modest refinements and qualifications made in order to do justice to differing perceptions concerning these basic styles. In labelling the styles the way I have, I am marrying the labels given to them by Bruce Jones on the one hand (representing a Christian understanding) and Alan Rowe and Richard Mason on the other (representing secular,

---

[23] Alan Rowe and Richard Mason, *Managing With Style*, 141, 155–8, 195–8.

corporate management thinking). The *autocratic* (Jones)-*directive* (Rowe, Mason) *style* is an extremely left brain way of leadership behaviour. It coincides with what others in the field call the *high directive style* and is characterized by being highly controlling, seeing things in black and white, and wanting a high degree of structure and predictability in a work situation.[24]

Hershey's and Blanchard's ground-breaking research approaches the different styles of leaders through the grids of how task-oriented or how relationship-oriented they are. However, Hershey and Blanchard are essentially coming to the same conclusions as other researchers in the field of management studies, but using different language (and perhaps evaluating differences more comprehensively than many others in the field). For them an autocratic-directive boss would fit in their quadrant under *high task and low relationship.*[25]

Task behaviour, as defined by them and the people whose pioneer studies they take steps further (e.g. of those involved in the Ohio State and Michigan State leadership behaviour research done between 1945 and 1965 roughly), means the extent to which leaders are probably to organize the roles and activities of the group they oversee.[26] On the other hand, relationship behaviour measures the extent to which leaders are probably to facilitate certain behaviour in the performance of a task by the group through building of personal relationships with group members,

---

[24] John D.W. Beck and Neil M. Yeager, *The Leader's Window: Mastering the Four Styles of Leadership to Build High-Performing Teams* (New York: John Wiley & Sons Inc., 1994), 25.

[25] Paul Hershey and Kenneth H. Blanchard, *Management of Organizational Behavior: Utilizing Human Resources* (Englewood Cliffs, NJ: Prentice Hall, 1993, 6th edition), 128–9.

[26] Ibid., 129.

whether through intensive communication or socio-economic support.[27]

Correspondingly, church growth consultant Callaghan maintains that there are four basic styles of church leaders: manager (or administrator); boss (or benevolent, authoritarian dictator); enabler (or developmental process planner); and charismatic inspirer (or motivator).[28] Obviously the 'boss' is the equivalent of the high task and low relationship style, or of the autocratic-directive style. In *Management for Your Church*, Lindgren and Shawchuck call this style *traditional* whereby that sort of leader maintains the traditions of the organization paternally and stands by the status quo.[29] Similarly, a Chinese-written book on intercultural studies views the four fundamental personality/style types as dominant (extrovert, task-oriented), influential (extrovert, person-oriented), steady (introvert, person-oriented), and competent (introvert, task-oriented).[30] As their way of determining personality types indicates, the dominant style would be congruent with the *autocratic-directive* style mentioned above.

In describing a high task and low relationship style leader (that is, an autocratic-directive one), we are looking at the stereotypical traditional leader. This is the profile of a 'born' or 'natural' leader. An extreme version of this style would be Saddam Hussein, who apparently

---

[27] Ibid.

[28] Kenon L. Callaghan, *Effective Church Leadership: Building on the Twelve Keys* (New York: HarperSan Francisco, 1990), 39.

[29] Alvin J. Lindgren and Norman Shawchuck, *Management for Your Church* (Nashville, TN: Abingdon, 1977), 26.

[30] Cecilia Yu, ed., *A Winning Combination: Understanding the Cultural Tensions in Chinese Churches* (Petaluma, CA: Chinese Christian Mission, 1986), 63.

likes to control every aspect of Iraqi government. But autocratic-directive leaders do not have to be dictators. They are needed in certain situations and for certain types of organizations. Who would want to serve in a war in a ground forces unit with a sergeant who polled everyone in the unit before making a decision? Autocratic-directive leaders are people who are 'action oriented and decisive and look for speed, efficiency, and results . . . Their focus is short range, and they tend to have the drive and energy needed to accomplish difficult tasks. They also focus on problems internal to the organization. Interestingly, they sometimes feel insecure and want status to protect their position.'[31]

The advantage of this style is that it possesses a clear sense of vision, and is resolute in doing what it takes to get the desired results, even if that means running over or using people in the process. Gangel calls this kind of leader *a driving style administrator* whom 'we often associate with strong, natural leadership'.[32] Illustrating this style of leadership is Al Dunlap, feared executive trouble-shooter. Reported on in *The Economist*, Dunlap took charge of seven companies on three continents in the past fifteen years, companies that were awash in red ink. He turned most of them around, mainly ones in the pulp and paper business. However, to accomplish these dramatic turnarounds he had been ruthless in reducing the companies' workforces, especially those in management. Assessing his personality traits, the columnist reporting on him says this: 'Watching him launch into a well-rehearsed tirade, it is hard to imagine him listening carefully to

---

[31] Alan Rowe and Richard Mason, *Managing With Style*, 45.

[32] Kenneth O. Gangel, *Feeding & Leading: A Practical Handbook on Administration in Churches and Christian Organizations* (Grand Rapids, MI: Baker Book House, 1989), 23.

dissenting views, or pausing to adapt his ideas to the facts at hand. Why would a busy executive learn what is best in a company, when he arrives already knowing what needs to be done? The same lack of self-doubt that makes Mr Dunlap so successful in the sickest firms would make such a man disastrous in most of the rest'.[33]

The down side of the autocratic-directive style, then, is that it requires intensive involvement by the leader (micro-management), which might be effective when a business or a ministry is small, or beginning, but which creates limitations on problem-solving ability over time and, as just insinuated, is not a very people-friendly style.[34] Commenting on the down side of this style too, Beck and Yeager say, 'A leader who is highly directive will be ineffective if team members have more information than the leader, already understand the situation clearly, know what needs to be done, and have already been taking appropriate action. In these situations, the leader is *dominating*, taking control when it is unnecessary, interrupting the effort of followers, and overriding their initiatives.'[35]

The analytical style

Also left brain, the *analytical style* is not actually represented in Jones' model – although he does acknowledge its existence through mentioning the Myers-Briggs' 'stabilizer' type – and so we will just use the Rowe and Mason designation to label it.[36] The analytical leader is

---

[33] 'Ready, Fire, Aim'. December 6, 1997, 74.

[34] John Beck and Neil Yeager, *The Leader's Window*, 52–3.

[35] Ibid.

[36] Cited in Bruce Jones, *Ministerial Leadership*, 106–112.

characterized 'by the tendency to overanalyze a situation or to always search for the best possible solution . . . People with this style often reach top posts in their companies, and while very technical in their outlook, they can often be autocratic . . . [They] want to be the best in [their] field, and [they] enjoy challenging assignments with considerable variety . . . Some people consider [the analyst] a little too disciplined and precise and that it takes [him or] her forever to make a decision.'[37]

Someone like the former American president Jimmy Carter comes to mind as being an analyst in style. While his successor, Ronald Reagan, liked to work from an uncrowded desk because he delegated well and so gave his time to more 'big picture' matters, Jimmy Carter was an engineer by training. He was notorious for holding up decisions because he wanted to read the proposed legislation or policy briefs in full. He wanted to consider every angle of a problem before giving his stamp of approval.

In the Hershey-Blanchard paradigm, the analytical leader is a *high relationship and high task behaviour* type of person. Perceived by followers, the analytical leader is 'seen as initiating more structure than is needed by the group and often appears not to be genuine in interpersonal relationships.'[38] According to Beck's and Yeager's four style paradigm, this is the *high direction and high support style*. A leader with this style 'is typified by direction from the top based on ideas that are actively solicited from the group . . . [and is] good at seeking information from key people and asking their opinions on issues'.[39] Nevertheless, the flip side of this style is that

[37] Alan Rowe and Richard Mason, *Managing With Style*, 46–7.
[38] Paul Hershey and Kenneth Blanchard, *Management of Organizational Behavior*, 132.
[39] John Beck and Neil Yeager, *The Leader's Window*, 25.

it can be over-involving and time-consuming for the participants subjected to this style of leadership. It fits in with the bureaucratic mindset and is more often seen in a second in command, like a Chief Accounting Officer (CAO), as opposed to a Chief Executive Officer (CEO), or a deacon, as opposed to an elder.

I'll never forget my years working in the shadows of Greg Livingstone, then US Director of Arab World Ministries, and subsequently the founder and president of Frontiers Mission, whose staff workers used to affectionately talk about the way they had to trail him picking up the pieces he left behind due to his whirlwind, visionary manner of leading. Never short on ideas, he was, conversely, not a manager. He was a conceptual and analyst style of leader. Rarely, as was true in his case, are the gift of management (administration) and the gift of leadership found in the same person.

Benevolent-autocratic conceptual style

Yet a third definitive style is the right brain one which we could call *benevolent-autocratic* (Jones) *conceptual* (Rowe and Mason). According to Rowe and Mason, what they call the conceptual style is characterized by 'creativity and a broad outlook, although [he or] she may rely too much on intuition and feelings. [He or] she is good at getting along with others, enjoys having discussions, and is willing to compromise. [He or] she is curious and open-minded but wants independence and dislikes following rules'.[40] Speaking of this style from a Christian viewpoint, Jones frames this leader as one who 'knows where he wants to go . . . He may lead with a strong hand, but he

---

[40] Alan Rowe and Richard Mason, *Managing With Style*, 48.

expresses a soft heart. He cares for people, not just programs and projects.'[41] What you have here is the *low task and low relationship* style of leader.[42] That is, the leader provides *low support and low direction* to the group.[43]

These are the delegators par excellence. They need to preoccupy themselves with getting in touch with the big picture. Not surprisingly, a close friend of mine, a mentor actually, in seeing my desk burdened down with a stack of paper work (although not disordered, I find myself needing to self-righteously add!), advised me to have a clear desk at all times. He would have gotten along well with Ronald Reagan! What he was really saying was that I should learn to delegate more so that I could give myself to seeing the forest clearly instead of being caught up in the trees! He was the founder of a successful and growing business with over three hundred employees. *Benevolent-autocratic conceptualizers* are 'seen as appropriately delegating to followers decisions about how the work should be done and providing little ... support where little is needed'.[44]

A leader with this style is Warren Buffett, the CEO of the holding company Berkshire Hathaway.[45] Famous for his aggressive acquisition style of corporate management, Buffett nonetheless is known by those close to him as one who will listen carefully to the managers of a new acquisition, preferring to cast himself as a consultant who will offer advice as needed but giving the existing

---

[41] Bruce Jones, *Ministerial Leadership*, 102.

[42] Paul Hershey and Kenneth Blanchard, *Management of Organizational Behavior*, 132.

[43] John Beck and Neil Yeager, *The Leader's Window*, 24.

[44] Paul Hershey and Kenneth Blanchard, *Management of Organizational Behavior*, 132.

[45] John Beck and Neil Yeager, *The Leader's Window*, 74–5.

leadership team freedom of movement to follow up on his suggestions and to solve their own problems. What is going on undoubtedly is that he is keen to more clearly grasp the big picture of the new acquisition and not to interfere unduly just to muddy the water at a time when he still has a steep learning curve to mount in order to grasp the essence of the company. The down side of this style is that, to some, a master delegator is simply downloading responsibility when more assertive leadership is called for. This style can appear to be shirking responsibility or being too abstract instead of action-oriented. While this style can appear to be people-friendly, it can also appear to be hypocritical; people may feel manipulated by this approach, even if they do not feel coerced, as they would be with the first style mentioned here.

Behavioural-democratic style

Finally, there is the more pronounced right brain leadership style we might call *behavioural* (Rowe and Mason)-*democratic* (Jones). Those manifesting this style are the people-friendly leaders – actually the sorts of people most churches come to expect to find in their pastors. Certainly you could argue that the behavioural-democratic individual personifies the leader with a shepherd's heart. He or she 'enjoys being with people and exchanging views with them . . . is a good listener and is interested in others. Executives with this style also are very supportive, are receptive to suggestions, show warmth, use persuasion, accept loose control, and prefer verbal to written reports. They tend to focus on short-run problems and are action-oriented.'[46]

---

[46] Alan Rowe and Richard Mason, *Managing With Style*, 49.

They are *high relationship and low task* leaders who are 'seen as having implicit trust in people and as being primarily concerned with their goal accomplishment'.[47] Such leaders are peace makers; they are consensus-builders and so frequently generate loyalty among their followers. They often make decisions not on the basis of whether they are intrinsically right or wrong but on how the decisions will affect and be perceived by those around them. Rightly or wrongly it has been observed that female executives are often more behavioural in their leadership style because they may have a greater capacity to be empathetic. Self-starters can be driven to distraction by this laissez-faire approach to leadership, on the other hand, because it is highly consultative and touchy-feely, thus slowing down the self-starter, who is entrepreneurial, and task-focused.

Only recently, McDonald's has had its golden arches become the most recognized logo world-wide, superseding the previous king of the commercial world, Coca-Cola.[48] Not far behind in sweeping the world by storm as a multi-national corporate giant is retailer Wal-Mart. Interesting it is to discover that a case can be made that its founder, Sam Walton, was a *behavioural-democratic* leader. He built his company on involvement and participation, starting with his family, with all major board decisions being made by consensus.[49] Obsessive about open communication, Walton passed on a legacy of company core values of openness, involvement, and shared responsibility.

---

[47] Paul Hershey and Kenneth Blanchard, *Management of Organizational Behavior*, 132.

[48] Thomas Sine, *Mustard Seed Versus McWorld: Reinventing Life and Faith for the Future* (Grand Rapids, MI: Baker Book House, 1999), 20.

[49] John Beck and Neil Yeager, *The Leader's Window*, 78–9.

While this style often works in Christian organizations, it can also be perceived as lacking integrity. Beck and Yeager put it this way: 'Listening to people's problems and giving them support can also be perceived as an *over-accommodating* style. Often leaders are too focused on relationships for their own sake. They try to be liked by everybody and keep everybody happy. They come across as friendly but are not well-respected.'[50]

Conclusion

What style of leader are you? The more you understand yourself, the better you are positioned to comprehend how those you lead perceive you. There is always a gap between our self-perception and others' perception of us. Effective leaders are able to see themselves objectively and so make the necessary adjustments in their behaviour to elicit desired responses from their co-workers. An invaluable way to gain further self-understanding is to take the MBTI or DSI tests as described in this chapter. Come what may, as we shall explore at more length in the duration of this book, ultimately servant leadership is not a function of style but of character. Since servanthood is a function of character, it will exhibit certain traits, traits which come naturally because they are consistent with your predominant leadership style, or traits that can be learned because you have the spirit of humility, and therefore of teachability, that humility being so characteristic of the Lord Jesus Christ himself. This, then, leads us to situational leadership, the topic of our next chapter.

---

[50] Ibid., 35.

2

Situational leadership is more than a secular buzzword

One of the fellows I golf with periodically waxes eloquent when we are striding down the fairway toward our golf balls, getting ready for the next shot. He insists that golf is a good object lesson for life. You could say the same thing about golf and leadership. You see, in every golf bag, there are various kinds of clubs. Drivers, which enable you to hit the ball considerable distances from the tee, about two to three hundred yards. Fairway irons, which enable you to hit the ball medium distances, but to a very precise distance, varying from about one to two hundred yards. Then there are the clubs to use close to the green or for special problems, like the sand wedge to hit the ball out of the sand trap, or the pitching wedge to hit the ball softly from the thick grass from 75 yards out onto the green close to the flag. Of course, finally there is the putter, which can only be used on the edge of or directly on the green, where the grass is close-cropped, so as to direct your ball most accurately toward the hole. Now the thing of it is that if you insist on using your three wood all the way down the course, you will find yourself possessing an astronomically high score – and in golf, the lower the score, the better. Different situations require different clubs. To say that golf is a foolish sport because all you are doing is chasing a little white ball around a lot of green real estate is to miss the strategy and skill involved in the game. Similarly, leadership requires that you use different styles and approaches according to the types of situations in which you are called upon to lead.

Situational leadership

What we are talking about here is situational leadership. The concept of situational leadership has become a very popular buzzword in secular management training circles. In essence, it critiques the traditional understanding of leadership development, which looks at the leader and the leader's followers. Added to those components, crucial as the first two are, according to situational leadership, is the context. Leadership is then said to be predictable on the basis of the interplay of these three factors: leaders, followers, and the situation. Therefore, differing situations require adjustable leadership styles. According to this theory, it is not enough to say that 'I have this way of leading, and everyone is going to have to do it my way, or the highway'. Leadership approaches can be modified because leaders are not only born, they are made.

An excellent overview of the history of viewing leadership situationally is found in Hershey's and Blanchard's book, *Management of Organizational Behavior: Utilizing Human Resources*, referred to repeatedly in the last chapter.[51] For example, they talk about Fred Fiedler's Leadership Contingency Model which describes three situational variables: (1) the leader's personal relations with members of the group; (2) the degree of structure in

---

[51] Especially see pages 116–39.

the task that the group has been assigned to perform; (3) the leader's power and authority as defined by the position he or she holds.[52] In this model eight different combinations of these three situational variables can occur, the most favourable one for leaders being where their group is one in which they are well-liked by the members, have a powerful position, and are directing a well-defined job. It can further be observed, for instance, that 'task-oriented' leaders tend to perform best in group situations that are black and white: either the group loves them or the group hates them. That knowledge in turn helps that kind of leader to get on with the job without there being any hidden agenda to worry about. In contrast, 'relationship-oriented' leaders tend to perform best in complex situations.

Likewise, highly structured group tasks, it has been found – such as making automobiles on an assembly line, require more 'high touch' and less task structure than more complicated but less structured group tasks – like developing ways to expand a business, a creative exercise, which may require the opposite approach. Thus, it is contended, the nature of the task should dictate the style of leadership.

That's not the end of the story though. Do not forget that situational leadership theory argues for there being *three* key factors in determining leadership style. The last chapter really only considered the innate style of the leader. It dealt with the style the leader unconsciously, in the sense of naturally, falls back on in dealing with the pressures and demands of leadership. So what is it we have not considered yet? The makeup of the followers, and the overall situation in which they work.

There are many more scenarios of leadership contexts once we introduce this next variable (the situation). For

---

[52] Ibid., 119–21.

example, a high relationship-low task style of leading works best with low capacity followers performing a highly structured task. They will need a lot of coaching and re-assurance to succeed in their task. Can you imagine, on the other hand, how high capacity (as in highly intelligent, well-educated, well-motivated) workers feel if their boss not only gives them a complex assignment but then fusses over them as if they were incompetent and needed to be hand-held as they creatively worked through the project to completion? Such followers need to be given the freedom to put their own stamp on things (low relationship) and given the sense that they can be left alone to do the job unless they call for their boss's problem-solving help. On the other hand, those same high capacity workers may need a little tender loving care to get through a simpler but time-consuming task, which, if they are not motivated to do by their boss, may lead to boredom and shoddy performance. According to Hershey and Blanchard, then, *a leader's style is deemed to be 'effective' or 'ineffective' according to how appropriate that style is in relation to the situation*. The situation includes both the type of task the group is called upon to accomplish and the type of group members who must be led.

Corresponding with Hershey's and Blanchard's landmark study are the findings of other leadership theorists, like John Gardener, who worked closely with several US presidents, who says,

Followers do like being treated with consideration, do like to have their say, do like a chance to exercise their own initiative – and participation does increase acceptance of decisions. But there are times when followers welcome rather than reject authority, want prompt and clear decisions from their leader, and want to close ranks around their leader. The ablest and most effective leaders do not hold to a single style. They may be highly supportive in personal relations when that is needed, yet capable of a quick, authoritative decision when the situation requires it.[53]

In like vein, Bennis and Nanus stress the importance of what they call 'organizational positioning', which they insist is the responsibility of the CEO to ascertain and plot as markets and economic conditions change.[54] As the world changes so quickly, how imperative it is for leaders to get a 'read' on how their firm's products or services will be received in the same way that navigators at sea periodically plotted their course by the stars to make sure their ship was not off course.

There are horror stories galore to bear testimony to the centrality of organizational positioning, of reading the market correctly or becoming uncompetitive or even bankrupt as a company in today's marketplace. International Harvester is one of the more sensational examples in recent memory. Famous for making farm machinery in North America, in 1981 it predicted a 1982 profit of $302 million. In actual fact, by the end of the 1982 fiscal year they had lost $1.64 billion, they misread the market trends so badly. By comparison, rival Caterpillar Tractor flourished. Not coincidentally, Caterpillar invested considerable money consistently in research and development.[55] Even more recently, the

[53] John Gardener, *On Leadership* (New York: The Free Press, 1993).

[54] Warren Bennis and Burt Nanus, *Leaders: The Strategies for Taking Charge*, (New York: Harper & Row, 1985), 155–6.

[55] Rosabeth Moss Kanter, *The Change Masters: Innovation & Entrepreneurship in the American Corporation* (New York: Simon & Schuster, 1984), 38.

overblown hype surrounding many of the high tech dot com companies has further underscored the relevance of including the context in which one leads as an essential component of leading effectively. At any rate, organizational positioning is Bennis' and Nanus' way of describing situational leadership. They focus more on the market environment (situation) end of things in doing so.

Or how about the reflections of leadership theorist Burns, who developed the bi-polar definition of leadership as being either transactional or transformational? Although he does not use the term 'situational leadership', Burns would associate that with his now famous phrase 'transformational leadership'. According to him, 'transforming leadership . . . recognizes and exploits an existing need or demand of a potential follower. But, beyond that, the transforming leader looks for potential motives in followers, seeks to satisfy higher needs, and engages the full person of the follower.'[56] In other words, the effective leader is the one who adjusts his or her style of leadership on the basis of the type of person who will be part of the team *and* the task or challenge to which these team members can be inspired to pursue.

Looking at situational leadership spiritually

What the secular world of corporations and management is now telling us is, surely, after all, a very biblical message. That is to say, not only that good leaders are the ones who have learned to adjust their style to fit the situation, but we would add that this is what servant leadership, as delineated in the Bible, is all about. Unselfish leading. By considering our followers first as we lead (thinking of

---

[56] James M. Burns, *Leadership* (Harper & Row, 1978), 4.

others as better than ourselves) and not insisting that they conform to our preferred way of doing things (for the sake of doing what it takes to build God's kingdom), we are demonstrating situational leadership at its best. Are we willing to adjust our style of decision making as leaders, I am saying, and thus indicating sensitivity to the Spirit's leading?

For a naturally directive style leader, to develop the art of listening to followers carefully before making decisions will not come easily but may make the difference between him or her being a successful pastor or not. Surely, this is what Paul has in mind when he exhorts: 'Live in peace with each other . . . Warn those who are idle, encourage the timid, help the weak, be patient with everyone' (1 Thess. 5:13b,14). Different strokes for different folks. The good shepherd calls each of his sheep by name (Jn. 10:3,4,14); he studiously determines their individual uniquenesses and therefore their needs ('Be sure you know the condition of your flocks; give careful attention to your herds' – Prov. 27:23).

Or what about jovial leaders who do not have a mean bone in their bodies but who nevertheless need to take the ministry to a decisive change of direction in order for it to survive, even though the drastic action may mean laying off some staff or relocating them? Painful change needs to happen more than infrequently in parachurch ministries, which often engage in self-preservating manoeuvering long after they have outlived their kingdom usefulness. Much institutionalism and stultification in Christian work can be traced to behavioural style leaders who are unwilling to risk unpopularity in order to make the tough decisions more easily made by conceptualizers (those who clearly see the big picture). A preponderance of extreme right brain leaders in Christian work can explain a tendency to avoid needed confrontation to resolve conflicts that dog the heels of many a ministry.

The importance of making situational adjustments is clearly seen in missionary work. Although I do not consider myself currently to be a missionary as I pastor a largely Canadian-born Chinese (CBC) congregation in the heart of Toronto, there are certain dimensions to it that cry out for cross-cultural sensitivity. At the same time, I observe the 'Great Wall of China' culturally between our various language-based congregations. The Cantonese one is made up primarily of older, well-settled immigrants who came to our shores in the immigration wave of the seventies and eighties, which was propelled by Hong Kong. In the nineties and since, the new immigration wave has been from mainland China. Those coming into our church now are found almost exclusively in our Mandarin congregation, although some come to the English one. The Mandarin converts and seekers seem to have almost no understanding of the Christian life and have to be dealt with at a much different level than the Cantonese who are well-established Christians even though they preserve many of their traditions that are quite related to a Confucian respect for family, authority, prescribed roles, and very conservative values. Not only do the CBCs of my congregation not speak with a discernible Chinese accent, they would be hard to distinguish from non-ethnic minority Canadians in their way of dressing (jeans are in at church!), slang, or even many of their other lifestyle values.

For someone to be in leadership in such a context, he or she needs to be something of a generalist – able to function in what amounts to being a multi-cultural (or layered cultural) setting. This is exactly what Cecilia Yu calls for in her edited book on Chinese Christians in North America. There it is noted, for example, that some differences in Chinese churches can be attributed to language and cultural differences whereas others may simply reflect differences of personality and therefore leaders have to be prepared to be flexible in leadership styles.[57] Summarizing the analysis are these thoughts, found to be in line with what we are saying about situational leadership.

> If language/culture and personality/work styles are correlated, we can conclude that every person, culturally Chinese or American, can learn to be a 'generalist' in the ministry: a task-oriented person can learn to build personal relationships; a relational person can learn organizational skills. Thus it would be profitable for an ABC [American-born Chinese] to spend some time immersing himself/herself in Chinese language and culture, perhaps as part of his/her seminary training; or an OBC [overseas-born Chinese] interning in an American church community, thus exposing himself/herself to more 'pure American' ways of life.
>
> We all have our limitations. But we can all stretch beyond them, with God's grace. Can we live with both our limitations and God's possibilities for us?[58]

Flexibility spells integrity?

Is such a chameleon-like adjustable leadership style consistent with integrity? Or does situational leadership camouflage hypocrisy? Or a manipulative spirit? Well, I think it depends on the attitude of the leader. Not being

---

[57] Cecilia Yu, ed., *A Winning Combination: Understanding the Cultural Tensions in Chinese Churches*, 62–8.
[58] Ibid., 66–7.

able to pin a leader down in terms of predictable behaviour can indeed be evidence of duplicity, of poor moral character. Nevertheless, if one reads Scripture carefully, whether considering the leadership behaviour of Moses, Jesus, or Paul, for example, you cannot confine their leading to one style each. Paul, for instance, knew how to be demanding and bold (witness his cajoling and chiding of the Galatian believers in Galatians 1:6 and 3:1, and his lambasting of their theological enemies in 5:12). He could also be vulnerable, wearing his feelings on his shirtsleeves, in his almost painfully vulnerable transparency with his spiritual offspring at Corinth: 'We have spoken freely to you, Corinthians, and opened wide our hearts to you. We are not withholding our affection from you, but you are withholding yours from us. As a fair exchange – I speak as to my children – open wide your hearts also' (2 Cor. 5:11–13). In both contexts, Paul is speaking as a leader, but his approach is entirely different in each case. In the first he is using a directive style, going so far as to appeal to his apostolic authority to compel compliance with his dictates. In the second case, he acts more out of his right brain, showing pastoral sensitivity to a church overwhelmed by grief at how they have had to discipline one of their own.

Moses was known to be an exceedingly humble man and yet he exhibited righteous indignation when he came down from Mount Sinai to see the Israelites succumbing to idolatry. Christ, who is described as being so gentle that he could not bruise a reed (a very tender plant), nonetheless had some very strong words for the religious establishment and was fearless in casting out the merchants from the Temple area. I like what Michael Green has to say about the necessity of a leader being flexible: 'Many men [leaders] are intransigent on peripheral matters, but soft at the centre. He should be the reverse. In fact, in a fast-changing social climate flexibility is essential; so is tenacious commitment to the faith.'[59] The spiritual leader instinctively knows what things to be dogmatic about and what things to be pliable about. A servant leader is a situational leader.

A pastor, Judson Edwards, calls this *the leadership paradox*.[60] Appearances can be deceiving. A pastor (and other types of Christian leaders) need to be many things to many people. Edwards even shows how secular leaders talk this language of seeming contradiction in leaders, quoting business consultant Richard Farson at one point, which I thought a very perceptive comment: 'Effective leaders and managers do not regard control as the main concern. Instead, they approach situations sometimes as learners, sometimes as teachers, sometimes as both. They trust the wisdom of the group. Their strength is not in control alone, but in other qualities – passion, sensitivity, tenacity, patience, courage, firmness, enthusiasm, wonder.'[61]

Different strokes for different organizations and churches too

Situational leadership is not only about different folks who need different strokes. The same flexibility is required in leading different types of churches and different types of Christian organizations. Each church or parachurch ministry has its own organizational culture.

[59] Michael Green, *Freed To Serve*, (Sevenoaks, UK: Hodder & Stoughton, 1983), 102.
[60] Judson Edwards, 'Turn It the Other Way', *Leadership* (Summer 1999), 41.
[61] Ibid.

While developing Arab World Ministries' presence in Canada, where it was hardly known in Christian circles at the time, and not having a large staff to work with, I steered it quite differently than I did Operation Mobilisation's work in Canada some years later. In the former case, I was more of a directive leader. I delegated little and put my stamp on almost every aspect of the ministry's evolution. However, with OM, I had a headquarters' staff of 12 people, regional full-time representatives, and an evangelistic ministry in Quebec involving more than twenty people full-time. In this latter CEO role, I had to develop more relational skills. We had some strong leaders and it was necessary to make many decisions on the basis of consensus-building. With OM's ethos of working by teams, OM encouraged a more democratic-collegial style of leadership. AWM, on the other hand, was full of independent-minded, tough tentmakers who were used to functioning individualistically. They had no problem with my style of leadership at the time. However, with a larger contingent of Generation X missionaries now in their ranks, it would be necessary to have a more high touch approach to overseeing them than that which I used over fifteen years ago.[62]

The well-known American evangelical author, Calvin Miller, is not known as much for his pastoring. In describing how he built a church from ten people to two thousand five hundred members, he made this interesting comment: 'I am the single greatest enemy to our [the church's] continued forward progress. At one plateau of membership size, I must relate to the church administration in one way. At a larger size,

---

[62] I currently serve on the International Council of Arab World Ministries as well as on its Canadian Board and so I am well aware of AWM's changing demographics.

I must vary my style of administration. Leadership adjustment is imperative in the long haul.'[63] He acknowledges here the necessity of situational leadership in Christian work.

Churches have their own character too. It is a wise pastor who scouts the terrain before pitching the tent. Lindgren and Shawchuck suggest there are five possible ways churches or organizations are run:

1. *The human relations way:* focuses on the need for persons to experience personal growth and to achieve their own personal goals in the institution – the institution is the servant of the people – theologically 'the fellowship of faith'
2. *The traditional way:* focuses on the achievement of institutional goals – people are servants of the institution – theologically 'the people of God'
3. *The systems approach:* holds that institutional goals and the growth of people are of equal importance – theologically the 'body of Christ'
4. *The charismatic approach:* rejects the status quo of the institution but the word of the leader dominates – theologically the 'new creation'
5. *The classical style:* focuses on the institution in a top-down bureaucratic method – people serve the institution – theologically 'God's building'

One can easily identify which organizational cultures prefer which styles of leadership. The human relations and the systems approaches lean toward right brain styles (people orientation) and the traditional, charismatic, and classical approaches gravitate toward left brain styles

---

[63] Calvin Miller, *Leadership: Thirteen Studies for Individuals or Groups* (Colorado Springs, CO: NavPress, 1987), 112.

(task orientation). Churches or ministries going through cataclysmic change will often prefer a charismatic leader, one who can rally the troops and issue forth 'God's word' *ex cathedra*.[64] In a crisis, people want the winsomeness of a warm PR style as found in a charismatic leader, but they also want clarity in direction because indecision breeds insecurity when the future is uncertain. A charismatic leader has both qualities: firmness and friendliness. Later on those same followers may revert to a previous expectation of the decision making process being highly participatory, expecting decisions to be made on a consultative basis. As Blanchard colourfully puts it: 'Sometimes people need direction, and lots of it. Sometimes they need support and direction. And perhaps sometimes they just need to be left alone.'[65]

It is also relatively easy to spot which style best describes a situational style of leadership: the systems approach. The systems approach is the style favoured by Lindgren and Shawchuck. Summarizing their promoting of this style, they theologize: 'Properly understood, a systems approach to church emphasizes the interrelationship of the prophetic (mission) and priestly (personal) roles with the kingly (managerial) role.'[66]

The systems approach especially takes the environment, that is, the context, seriously. This is true whether we are talking about the business world in the marketplace or in Christian circles. The environment of the workers, the environment of the marketplace (the customer) and the environment of the task. No wonder one-time CEO of Hewlett Packard, John Young, could say, 'Successful

[64] Kenon Callaghan, *Effective Church Leadership*, 69.

[65] Kenneth Gangel, *Feeding and Leading*, 22.

[66] Alvin Lindgren and Norman Shawchuck, *Management for Your Church*, (Nashville, TN: Abingdon, 1978) 137–8.

companies have a consensus from top to bottom on a set of overall goals. The most brilliant management strategy will fail if the consensus is missing.'[67] Much the same thesis is developed in Kanter's ground-breaking research project on scores of Fortune five hundred companies in the USA so as to reveal how their organizational culture could be used as an index to ascertain whether they would remain competitive in the years to come – and that culture determined what sort of leaders these successful companies attracted and/or would need in order to survive into the future.[68] Top-down management just does not sit well in the complex, well-educated, and rapidly-changing world we find ourselves in today. Ergo situational leadership. Ergo servanthood leadership.

Building a synergistic leadership team

Realizing that different situations and changing needs require different styles of leadership also tells us that leadership needs to be shared. A team approach to leading enables the total needs of the church or the organization to be addressed adequately. We will talk more about that in the chapter on *affability*. The fact is that virtually every group of people, whether they live in a mission compound at a Bible College in Africa or form an inner city church in a world class European city, needs the same range of personalities, spiritual gifts, and leadership styles. The leader with the driving vision needs the stability and patience of the administrative leader; the friendly elder needs the analytical business acumen of

---

[67] Quoted in Warren Bennis and Burt Nanus, *Leaders: The Strategies for Taking Charge*, 92.

[68] Rosabeth Moss Kanter, *The Change Masters*.

the deacon; the emotional entrepreneur needs the quiet helpfulness of the follower. Plurality in leadership is a biblical concept (as we shall develop later on) and is tailor-made for effective situational leadership. The good leader recognizes that only to some extent can he or she be all things to all people and so must learn to 'lead to his strength and staff to his weakness'.[69]

Roles do not always come in neat packages

Just as fluidity in leadership roles is demonstrated through the plural approach to leadership, so we are living in the *real* world by admitting that what we are asked to do as leaders does not always come in neat packages. One of the biggest complaints of pastors is that they were never told in seminary how much administration they would be expected to do in the pastorate. That explains why almost every Doctor of Ministry programme I know of, in North America at least, has one or more courses offered in the management of the local church.[70] Roles do not always come in neat packages which is why we must avoid being stereotypical about what we can expect from our leaders.

Currently there is a lot of emphasis on bifurcating the leadership and management roles and a concomitant assigning of these complementary roles to different

---

[69] Kenneth Gangel, *Feeding and Leading*, 25.

[70] The Doctor of Ministry degree is considered to be the highest professional degree attainable by the pastor, as opposed to the PhD in theology or biblical studies or philosophy, for instance, which is more concerned with adding to the body of knowledge academically in that field of study, and meant to prepare one for teaching in that specialized field.

people.[71] However, the leader is expected to give attention to detail at times. And the manager is expected to buy into and sell the overarching vision. Therefore, I am being slightly contrary in calling for avoidance of too neatly separating the roles, agreeing with Gardener in his analysis.

> Even the most visionary of leaders is faced on occasion with decisions that every manager faces: when to take a short-term loss to achieve a long-term gain, how to allocate scarce resources, whom to trust with a delicate assignment. So even though it has become conventional to contrast leaders and managers, I am inclined to use slightly different categories, lumping leaders and managers/leaders into one category and placing in the other category those numerous managers whom one would not normally describe as leaders.[72]

Realistically, more than one spiritual gift is required to exercise the role of leadership. The tests that I have taken show me to have a blend of spiritual gifts that can be characterized by *leadership*, *management*, and *teaching*. This combination of spiritual gifts is what Bobby Clinton in his leadership literature refers to as the *gift mix* – and that is unique to everyone in the body of Christ and to every leader, I might add. Various gifts exercised in a multitude of ministries produce a variety of effects. That's the genius of our creative and powerful God. What we tend to find is that, as needs vary, so do our ministries and perhaps our gifts. Notwithstanding the non-rigidity with which we should reflect on how God uses us, we should specialize and discover our niche as

---

[71] See for example the way Burt Nanus and Stephen Covey do so in, respectively, *Visionary Leadership* (San Francisco: Jossey-Bass, 1992), and *Principle-Centered Leadership*.

[72] John Gardener, *On Leadership*, 4.

we discern, through the trials and errors, the ups and downs, of ministry, just what it is we are cut out for in the way of serving the Lord. As Scottish Olympic track medallist Eric Liddell, of *Chariots of Fire* movie fame, declared, when asked why he kept up his competitive running when his Christian faith seemed to interfere with it, 'I was made to run'. So should we discover what we are uniquely made to do, and 'go for it'.

Conclusion

Is it putting too much pressure on leaders to expect them to change their natural way of leading all the time? Why should people with outstanding capabilities, the King Sauls standing head and shoulder above their countrymen, have to go with the flow? Well, all I will question at this juncture is why leaders should be treated as a privileged class. Everyone else has to slave away to become excellent in their profession or field of service. Doctors have to keep up with their medical journals. Systems analysts and computer programmers seem to have a perpetual steep learning curve. It was said of General MacArthur's exploits and tactical brilliance in the Pacific theatre of World War Two that his qualities and successes were the product of a lifetime of study and action. Similarly, it could be argued that Ronald Reagan's amazing communication skills as USA president were the product of many decades of acting.

Bennis and Nanus describe five myths about leadership. Two of them are germane to this discussion. The first is that leadership is a rare skill (which implies that leaders are born and cannot be made). The second myth is that leaders are born and cannot be made, and so they say, 'The truth is that major capacities and competencies of leadership can be learned . . . Furthermore, whatever natural endowments we bring to the role of leadership, they can be enhanced.'[73] Along the same lines, Gardener contends that 'most of what leaders have that enables them to lead is learned. Leadership is not a mysterious activity. It is possible to describe the tasks that leaders perform. And the capacity to perform those tasks is widely distributed in the population.'[74]

The fact of the matter is that each of us is in process. That means we do change, whether we are consciously aware of it or not. In my conversations with various types of fellow leaders over the years I have been struck how many have alluded to their admitting to drifting more and more into the centre and away from extremes in their style(s) of leadership. If the truth were known, I did not lead AWM differently than OM for purely theoretical or intentional reasons. I was more directive when I was younger because I was still learning about myself, about God, about other people . . . and about leadership. As Brouwer says in his classic management article,

> Human beings constantly change their behavior, as we see if we examine ourselves (and others) critically enough. . . Change in behavior is constant.
>
> The difficulties managers have in thinking about changes in behavior come from their inability to detect change, and from fuzzy thinking behind such comforting, though fallacious, notions as, 'You can't teach an old dog new tricks,' 'He was born that way,' or 'He's been like that ever since I've known him.'[75]

---

[73] Warren Bennis and Burt Nanus, *Leaders: The Strategies for Taking Charge*, 222.

[74] John Gardener, *On Leadership*, XIX.

[75] Paul J. Brouwer, 'The Power To See Ourselves', *Harvard Business Review* (November/December 1964), 37.

Can you imagine how boring it would be if we were all one kind of leader? If servant leadership would always wear the same face? Nevertheless, while servant leadership can be expressed in all four leadership styles of directive, analytical, conceptual, and behavioural, there are characteristics that cut across all leadership styles in the sense of their needing to be found in servant leaders, no matter what their inherent or contextualized style of leadership. To those common strands of behaviour in servant leaders we now turn in the second main section of the book. In a sense, you can say that the embracing of these practical, discernible qualities, no matter whether they fit in with your preferred style of leading, identifies you as being situational in your leadership. That situational approach to your leadership in turn singles you out as being a servant leader. I think Longenecker is striving to say much the same thing as I am when he puts it this way: 'Temperament patterns are designed to create welcome diversity in what would otherwise be a hideously bland church, but they are never an excuse for side stepping, minimizing, or ignoring the Bible's relational standards. All Christian leaders, regardless of personality type or temperament pattern, are under the same obligations.'[76]

---

[76] Harold Longenecker, *Growing Leaders by Design*, 112.

3

Accessibility: Please walk on the grass

Not by accident in 1999 was Toronto named the 'greenest' world class city. Awarded this honour by the United Nations for any city of three million or more inhabitants that had the most open spaces and parkland for its masses, Toronto deserves the distinction. Symbolic of its user-friendly and habitable environs is the familiar sign posted in some of its parks, 'Please walk on the grass'. Whether one is jogging for miles on the Don Trail alongside a busy motorway, or golfing in the heart of the city with the subway[77] forming one boundary and high-rise buildings the others, there is this sense that Toronto doesn't take itself too seriously but seeks to remind its citizens that there is a bigger world out there, one that takes its frame of reference from what is more than artificial. In the same way, a servant leader shows humility by not sanitizing him or herself from the world of followers. One of the premier marks that distinguishes an authentic servant leader from a wannabe is the leader's availability, or accessibility, to the average person in the pews or front lines.

Apart from George Verwer's transparency, there is no quality of his leadership that ties *(tys)* him more to

---

[77] The 'subway' in North America is what is called the 'underground' in Great Britain.

servanthood than his accessibility to people in the trenches. I had only been several months with OM in India in the early 1970s when I received a personal letter from George Verwer, even though OM had over a thousand workers at the time. This was back in the days when personalized, computer-generated letters were unknown. The white-out corrections of the hand-typed letter made it abundantly clear that George had dictated the letter personally. It was the real McCoy!

In subsequent years, whenever I had the occasion to be at an OM conference where he was in attendance or visit an area where he was present – like the times when he sailed on board the LOGOS when it carried out evangelism port to port around India (to this day he is banned from entering India) – he always singled me out to spend personal time with him, as I came on board from the inland teams. I was no one special because I observed that he spent quality time with a host of OMers, OM graduates, and people from the general Christian public. Not only that, but I observed (and experienced first-hand) that he was not above spending significant quantities of time with leaders he was seeking to mentor or influence. On more than one occasion George spent half a day or more with me, talking and praying. His usual practice was to take me on one of his long walks. Over the years, whether inside OM or out, I have had those famous walks with him in locales as diverse as England, Canada, the Netherlands, and Nepal. From his example more than any other, I learned the importance of a leader spending time with his or her people.

Unfortunately, too frequently in Christian circles there has been this tendency to ape the world by leaders posturing themselves as being important through the way they surround themselves with evangelical Secret Service equivalents who keep distance between their guru and an adoring public. Christian celebrities are whisked from limousines to powder rooms to stages and back to waiting limousines which take them to private hotel rooms before you can shake a stick. The idea is that the leader's time is more precious than anyone else's and so he or she must be protected from ordinary people, who would only waste their time. One wonders how that squares with the example of the Lord Jesus who did not come to be served but to serve and who was in the habit, as it says in John 3:22, of 'spending time with [his disciples]' (NASB).

The danger of isolation

It is fascinating to see that secular leaders are now recognizing the impact they can make by mingling with the average worker. Among the first to chronicle this practice was Thomas Peters and Robert Waterman in their bestseller, *In Search of Excellence*, wherein they described this accessibility of the leader to the common person. Commenting on this tendency of leaders to isolate themselves from their employees, they observed: 'One of the problems in American companies is the reluctance of the chief executive officer to get out and travel, to listen to criticisms. There's a tendency to become isolated, to surround himself with people who won't argue with him.'[78]

An example of this sort of leader in the business world who makes a special effort to stay connected is Rupert Murdoch, the owner of the third largest communication

---

[78] Thomas J. Peters and Robert H. Waterman, *In Search of Excellence: Lessons from America's Best-Run Companies* (New York: Warner Books, 1982), 290.

business globally, including Star-TV. He is said to run his business by phone, thus keeping in constant touch with his people.[79]

The example of Jesus

In a simple yet profound study of the way Jesus went about training the Twelve, the Indian Christian leader, Chandapilla, has a whole chapter devoted to Jesus' availability to his disciples.[80] The heart of this quality, in his view, was that Christ simply physically placed himself at his disciples' disposal. He was a constant presence with them – whether enjoying a wedding, resting, eating and drinking, praying, mourning the loss of a friend, or preaching in Judea's villages. The disciples were able to observe first-hand his response to their times of joy (Luke 19:37), times of helplessness (Mark 9:17–20), and times of fear (John 6:19,20). The result? The disciples responded enthusiastically to his leadership: 'The quality of availability in a leader is that ability in him whereby he creates full confidence in the trainees toward his own self by putting himself fully at their disposal and placing his confidence in them.'[81]

Whether at the individual level (e.g. with Peter in Mark 1:30,31; Luke 22:31), or at the group level (e.g. Mt. 17:17), Jesus always seemed to have time for people. Although Jesus seemed to have priority relationships within an inner circle (witness his taking of only Peter, James and John to the Mount of the Transfiguration), he

---

[79] William Shawcross, *Murdoch* (New York: Simon & Schuster, 1994).

[80] P.T. Chandapilla, *Jesus The Master Trainer* (Bombay: Gospel Literature Service, 1985), 33–38.

[81] Ibid., 33.

gave himself without reserve to them all. In fact, apart from the Twelve, Jesus had an outer circle of 72 disciples (Luke 10:1,17), and was followed by 'multitudes' (Luke 14:25). But it was the 12 disciples in particular who came to him about all sorts of problems, whether spiritual (who had authority to minister in the name of Jesus, Mark 9:38–41) or practical (no food to eat, John 4:27–33), thus demonstrating that they had a comfort zone with him enhanced by frequent exposure to him on a personal basis.

This 'up close and personal' dynamic in Jesus' relationship with his followers is surely what enabled the apostle John to say what he did at the beginning of his letter, 1 John: 'That which was from the beginning, which we have heard, which we have seen with our eyes, which we have looked at and our hands have touched – this we proclaim concerning the Word of life.' Jesus led through accessibility. That is servant leadership.

Paul's example

Turning to another excellent biblical example of accessibility, the apostle Paul is instructive. Paul was individually called by God to a major leadership role in the early church, but he was not a lone ranger as he conducted his ministry. He perhaps had the first international mission team, which we read about in Acts 20:4! Especially at the end of his letters, we learn from his practical directions that he was sur-rounded by those who could carry out ministry tasks in conjunction with him. Phoebe is talked about in this way in Romans 16:2; John Mark, Justus, Priscilla and Aquila, Timothy, Urbanus, Demas, and Luke were described as Paul's 'fellow workers' (Col. 4:10,11; Rom. 16:3,9,22; Phlm. 24); Aristarchus, Andronicus, Junias and Epaphras were imprisoned with Paul (Col. 4:10; Rom. 16:7;

Phlm. 23); Tychicus was a 'faithful minister and fellow servant' (Col. 4:7); Erastus and Artemas could be 'sent' on a mission (2 Tim. 4:20; Tit. 3:12). As Longenecker puts it: 'Some were with Paul almost continually. We can speak as easily of "Paul and his men" as of "Jesus and His men".'[82] Paul led through being accessible and so he too demonstrated thereby to being a servant leader.

Interruptions

Indicative of a capacity to serve others through availability is a willingness to be interrupted in the midst of a busy schedule. Known as a careful time manager, I must confess that in my early years of leadership, I tried to curtail people's access to me by fitting them into prescribed appointment times so that I would not be 'wasting time'. I also developed my own techniques for reducing the amount of time people 'interfered' with my carefully-laid plans for each day. These included standing up from my desk and starting slowly to walk toward the door when I had had enough of their interruption! Or I sent out the non-verbal signal 'you are not wanted here' by shuffling my papers on my desk when I began to get impatient with the chit-chat. Increasingly though I became convicted, as I read the gospels repeatedly, by the example of Christ, who demonstrated an incredible ability to be flexible and patient, and knew that I needed to develop more sensitivity to people. Typical of Christ's availability in the midst of a hectic schedule is the episode described in Mark 1:32–39.

> That evening after sunset the people brought to Jesus all the sick and demon-possessed. The whole town gathered at the

---

[82] Harold Longenecker, *Growing Leaders by Design*, 76.

door, and Jesus healed many who had various diseases. He also drove out many demons, but he would not let the demons speak because they knew who he was.

Very early in the morning, while it was still dark, Jesus got up, left the house and went off to a solitary place, where he prayed. Simon and his companions went to look for him, and when they found him, they exclaimed: 'Everyone is looking for you!'

Jesus replied, 'Let us go somewhere else – to the nearby villages – so that I can preach there also. That is why I have come.' So he travelled throughout Galilee, preaching in their synagogues and driving out demons.

There are several contrasts that attract our attention in this passage. Evidently Jesus was a busy man! It is only after sunset, first of all, that the people in the town brought their sick to him (v. 32). Notice that they brought *all* their sick and demon-possessed. To have a look at all of them would have been time-consuming, to say the least, and not done at a time of day when Jesus would have been at his sharpest. To emphasize the stressfulness of the scene, the next verse indicates that the *whole* town appeared on his doorstep. After such a hectic schedule, little wonder that we find him the next morning, then, slipping away to get some private space (v. 35). Perhaps the only way he could be assured of time alone was to disappear 'very early in the morning, while it was still dark'.

Typical of many non-leaders is an insensitivity to the pressures of leadership. Hence it is not surprising to find Simon Peter leading his gang out to Jesus to make sure Jesus doesn't enjoy any 'down time' (v. 36). Speaking from experience, I have found that I can always count on certain parishioners calling me on my day off each week. As if to ensure that Jesus would feel guilty about not being available 24 hours a day seven days a week, Peter had to chide Jesus that everyone was looking for him. Notwithstanding the disciples' self-absorption and disregard for Jesus' emotional and spiritual needs, Jesus was responsive to their agenda. He demonstrated flexibility in agreeing to join them in ministry again right away, thus exhibiting the sort of unselfishness that ought to be associated with the servant leader. When one is extremely busy and blocking off time for self-renewal, but accessible, you know that that person is not the type who feeds off being around other people all the time, but is remaining flexible at great personal cost. There is the sort of person who remains resilient by being around people. Such a character will find any excuse to avoid being alone. That Jesus constantly alternated quiet time with his heavenly Father with the demands of a busy schedule suggests that he was not of that personality type (see again the same blend of people-intensive ministry with seeking of solitude in the remaining verses of this same chapter in Mark – verses 40–45).

Another famous figure notable for his willingness to interrupt a busy schedule to make time for individuals was Mahatma Gandhi. A strict disciplinarian, Gandhi was known for such daily routines as walking three to four miles, weaving (spinning) half an hour, answering every letter in a voluminous correspondence personally, and being punctual for a steady stream of appointments with politicians and others. Yet it was common for him to break away from his schedule to see someone who arrived on his doorstep asking for an audience. For instance, in the midst of intense negotiations with the British in 1946, he took out 15 minutes to talk to a crippled young woman who appeared at the Satyagraha Ashram in Gujarat he called home.[83]

---

[83] Louis Fischer, *Gandhi: His Life and Message for the World* (New York: Mentor Books, 1960), 128–129.

Should it surprise us, then, as management studies become more of a science, to find that effective secular executives spend the bulk of their time with people, and that much of that time is unstructured? For instance, Deutschman's study found that only twenty per cent of a CEO's time is pre-booked, even though seventy per cent of his or her time is spent with people.[84]

What you are signalling to your people when you allow them to interrupt you (within limits) is that you are not in the business of controlling them but, if anything, of being controlled by them. Stephen Covey understands this principle at work when he makes this comment: 'When you fully empower people, your paradigm of yourself changes. You become a servant. You no longer control others; they control themselves. You become a source of help to them.'[85]

As we shall see in more depth in the next chapter, such high touch leadership has moved beyond a single-minded task orientation to a people orientation. As one pastor explained it, becoming people-oriented was a matter of shifting from a preoccupation with the functional to the relational.[86] Oh yes, we want to be sure we are results-driven in our leadership. But what about the results in people's lives when you treat them as having significance and not just being pawns in the game called 'church' or 'ministry'? It was not until I felt that I had matured beyond a simple task orientation in my leadership – marked by carefully-crafted mission statements and quantifiable goals – that I dared to take steps to enter the pastoral ministry. I

[84] Alan Deutschman, 'The CEO's Secret of Managing of Time', *Fortune* (June 1, 1992), 65–74.
[85] Stephen Covey, *Principle-Centered Leadership*, 256–257.
[86] Wayne Schmidt, 'Sharing Goals and Life', *Leadership* (Summer 1999), 101.

had been in missions' parachurch leadership roles for seventeen years by then! Yes, this book is all about servant leadership for slow learners – and I have been one of them!

Modelling

We're not talking here about walking down a runway to display designer fashions! Accessibility implies that an example can be set. Perhaps the most powerful yet under-valued aspect of discipling and equipping others is through modelling the Christian life. To be able to do this suggests that the one setting the example can be observed closely and constantly. Modelling is highly motivational for followers, as any smart leader knows. Ed Dayton defines modelling as being 'a conscious effort on the part of the leader to speak and act in such a way that when he or she is emulated by followers their actions will be recognized by the leader as being appropriate and honoring to Christ'.[87] As we have remarked, Jesus *lived* among his disciples. Paul could say, 'Be imitators of me' because he allowed himself to be put under the micro-scope of daily exposure (Phil. 3:17; 1 Tim. 4:11–14; 2 Tim. 2:15; Titus 2:6–8). Especially in Christian work, we need to intentionalize our training of leaders in this way because we cannot, generally speaking, go out and hire top talent, for one thing. Nevertheless, Peter Drucker, considered to be the father of modern management theory, could say this about the necessity of example in any setting: 'Management is largely by *example*. Executives who do not know how to make themselves effective in their own job and work set the wrong example.'[88]

---

[87] Ed Dayton, 'Modelling', *Christian Leadership Letter* (July 1978), 1.
[88] Peter Drucker, *The Effective Executive*, 523.

The exposure of oneself to followers/employees lets these people determine what your values really are. It is not what the leader says he or she believes but how he or she behaves that determines in people's minds what is really believed. Peters and Waterman put it this way in their analysis of state of the art companies: 'Probably few of us would disagree that actions speak louder than words, but we behave as if we don't believe it. We behave as if the proclamation of policy and its execution are synonymous.'[89] Just to take one example, how the executive or pastor uses his or her time is actually closely watched by others because the use of time is a symbol of priorities. Is he or she a workaholic? Is there time set aside for the spouse? Is there time taken to stop and smell the roses? Are holidays enjoyed? Does he or she eat lunch at the desk while working? Can you walk into your boss's office unannounced? Portraying in action what we teach verbally is the method of modelling Jesus used. His praying alone led his disciples to ask him to teach them to pray (Luke 11:2–4). His feet washing led them to understand what he meant by servant leadership (John 13:1–17).

Just as the craftsmen of the Middle Ages had their apprentices, as leaders in today's world we need to allow people to be around us as we work, if for no other reason than because of the power of our example. John Wesley knew the wisdom of this approach to leadership training. Seldom travelling by horseback alone, he deliberately took preachers along so they could observe him up close, thus learning from him.[90] He also listened to these companions

---

[89] Thomas Peters and Robert Waterman, *In Search of Excellence*, 73.
[90] Howard Snyder, *The Radical Wesley and Patterns for Church Renewal* (Pasadena, CA: WIPF & Stock Publishers, 1996), 163–164.

preach and critiqued their messages for them. Effective leaders are trained when this kind of exposure to a veteran leader is forthcoming. Known for integratively training nationals in Sri Lanka, in this regard, Ranjit DeSilva maintains that 'though spiritual formation can be achieved in a variety of ways, it demands a one-to-one relationship between trainer and trainee'.[91] The bottom line is that when people have the opportunity to see that our actions match our verbosity, they view us as having integrity. Integrity is the quality that the former US president, Dwight Eisenhower, said was supreme for the leader.[92]

To be available to people to this extent is costly. It will not be engaged in for long without one having a real desire for the well-being of others, that is, a servant heart. Paul had this people-focused approach to leadership, which is why we hear him say to the Thessalonians: '. . . we were gentle among you, like a mother caring for her little children. We loved you so much that we were delighted to share with you not only the gospel of God but our lives as well, because you had become so dear to us' (1 Thess. 2:7,8). The word translated as 'gentle' in verse seven is *epioi*, which is a botanical term describing the careful nurturing of a young plant so that it grows properly to maturity.[93]

One of the most positive spin-offs of rubbing shoulders with servant leaders, that is, with those who allow you sufficient access to them, is that they become a model for you in their vision, which, almost by osmosis, sharpens yours.[94] Through formal settings, such as in a

---

[91] Ranjit DeSilva, 'The Missing Ingredient in Leadership Training,' *Evangelical Missions Quarterly* (January 1996), 50.
[92] Harold Longenecker, *Growing Leaders by Design*, 131.
[93] Ted Engstrom, *The Fine Art of Mentoring* (Brentwood, TN: Wolgemuth & Hyatt, 1989), 177.
[94] Harold Longenecker, *Growing Leaders by Design*, 66.

board meeting, in combination with connecting while in informal settings, such as over a cup of tea, the servant leader seeks to impart his or her passion for ministry. Joseph D'Souza, leader of OM's work in India, strikes me as being one of the up and coming two-thirds world mission leaders who is skilled at this type of modelling. (Two-thirds world delineates the approximately two-thirds of the world's population and land mass in the continents of Latin America, Asia, Africa and Oceania.) He likes to hold several days of national leaders' meetings annually in which his top fifty or so leaders of a work comprised of seven hundred national missionaries come together to brainstorm and pray together. On either side of those meetings, he spends time with these leaders one-on-one too. Joseph has a wonderful knack of grasping the big picture, a sense of how the Holy Spirit is leading OM-India forward, and an uncanny ability to articulate that vision without seeming to force it on anyone, all the while being inclusive. Everyone feels free to give their input although Joseph tends to control the outcomes. Studies have shown that two-thirds world people tend to be more relational in how they go about making decisions even as they defer to authority more readily than westerners. That is, they are concerned as much by how their decisions will affect and be received by their followers as they are about making the intrinsically right decisions.

Christian leaders in a postmodern world will increasingly have to function with this mindset in order to be effective. As we are seeking to demonstrate, people-friendly leading is not unbiblical nor ineffective, anyway. The upshot of this modelling is that we train leaders. It is not that time-consuming a task, but is rather more one of intentionalizing our availability to people for the sake of developing them, knowing the power of example. Longenecker has much the same grasp of this type of leadership training when he says the following.

> Is it [developing leaders] hard to do? The work is demanding because all ministry is demanding, but it's not impossible. A commitment to grow leaders does not call for another ten hours per week on top of an already busy schedule. What is required is a change in perspective! The same tasks are done and the same ministry performed, but with an eye to the effect on others. Take men with you as you serve; spend time with them, give them opportunities to watch, to be there, to learn, and as you create the climate, leaders appear.[95]

This method of influencing people by example is behind my periodic involvement on one of our church's several baseball teams. Our church participates in a church league which has over thirty teams in it. The games can get pretty competitive. One might ask why at the age of fifty I would be so foolish as to play in a team sport, twenty years past my prime! The simple reason is that, as much as I love the game of baseball, it gives me an opportunity to mix with many whom I am seeking to equip as future leaders. They need to be able to relate to me in 'normal' settings as well as in 'church' settings. Can a Christian have fun? Can one be competitive without it overriding courtesy, honesty, and fair play? Observing me live out my faith in different contexts enables them, hopefully, to learn from me.

Could it be that one reason leaders tend to be somewhat remote from the people they are leading is that they are afraid to have their life examined too

---

[95] Ibid., 148.

closely? This amusing little saying makes much the same point, as it describes different stages of a leader's career: the **go** stage – 'I do'; the **show** stage – 'Do as I do'; the **know** stage – 'Do as I did'; the **woe** stage – 'We are not saying or doing anything anymore'.[96]

We hear a lot about mentoring these days. An obvious question at this juncture is whether modelling as a method to train leaders is the same as mentoring. I would contend that modelling is similar to but different from mentoring, although both require a strong dose of being accessible to others in order to work. What then is mentoring? And how does it relate to this overarching servanthood principle of accessibility to people?

Mentoring

Much has been written in the last decade about this subject. Fundamental to distinguishing between modelling and mentoring is the understanding that there is more selectivity implied in mentoring than in modelling. We can't spread ourselves too thin or we become good for nothing – and for nobody! Mentoring is what Barnabas did with Saul of Tarsus, who without the son of encouragement's quality input could not have become a Paul! No doubt Barnabas had other irons in the fire; he was active in the early church, we know. His name appears as early as Acts 4 where we see him donating property to the church in Jerusalem. Certainly if he was known as an encourager, he was very relational in his ministry (e.g. consider his handling of John Mark) and

---

[96] Richard Sharp, 'Modelling It: If You Don't Model It, They Won't Do It!', *FrontLine* (August/September 1992), 31.

yet he zeroed in on Saul, a new convert, in a special way. It is this latter way he influenced people that we call mentoring. It involves special time, prayer and emotional energy – in a word, genuine interest in the person being mentored. Different it is from discipleship in that while discipling involves the imparting of basic spiritual disciplines, there is more of an emotional attachment connected with mentoring, and it is kind of a second level of discipling.

Those who have a sound track record of mentoring advise that one should only consider mentoring several people at most. Reflecting on my own current situation, I seek to influence people as a Christian leader in a number of different ways. I preach from the pulpit every Sunday morning and so influence about two hundred people. I also teach adult Christian Education[97] every other semester, which will allow for more personal interaction with attendees, who usually number about fifty. I also work with about twelve people on the church board, including doing some training sessions with them from time to time, apart from our monthly business meetings. Then I am in a pastoral team mutual accountability relationship with three other men. This latter relationship I consider to be more of a mentoring one. These men have more access to me on a personal level than those in any of the other teaching or training relationships. They would fit into the sort of mentoring arrangement that is sometimes referred to as 'peer mentoring'. I can learn as much from them as they can from me. Then there are a couple of promising young men who show leadership potential whom I spend personal time with on a regular basis, and so have a sort of mentoring connection with. This

---

[97] A fancy, more contemporary, name for Sunday School!

kind of mentoring Hans Finzel labels as 'downward mentoring'.[98]

In like manner, Chuck Colson of Prison Fellowship seeks to be held accountable by his peer mentors by voluntarily requesting that someone from his board, whom he respects, periodically reviews his expense accounts, his calendar and his priorities.[99] Accountability and peer mentoring can involve somewhat interchangeable relationships.

Is mentoring for everybody just because he or she wants to exhibit servanthood in their leadership style? Not according to Bobby Clinton, Christian leadership theorist, teaching at Fuller Theological Seminary in California, who says: 'Not everybody is suited to be a mentor. Mentors are people who can readily see the potential in a person. They can tolerate mistakes, brashness, abrasiveness, etc. in order to see potential develop. They are flexible and patient, recognizing that it takes time and experience for a person to develop. They have vision and ability to see down the road and suggest next steps a protégé needs for development.'[100]

Mentoring, then, although it doesn't have to be called such, involves a deliberate singling out of someone whom you feel will deserve special attention. It may not just consist of giving quality time to that person but doing

---

[98] Hans Finzel, *The Top 10 Mistakes Leaders Make* (Wheaton, IL: Victor Books, 1994), 168. Finzel also adds to his list *internal peer mentoring* which is similar to my *peer mentoring* above in that it involves those at roughly the same level within the organization, or in my case, church. He also adds *external peer mentoring*, which is akin to internal peer mentoring but with those outside one's place of employment or direct ministry circle.

[99] H. B. London and Neil B. Wiseman, *The Heart of a Great Pastor: How To Grow Strong and Thrive Wherever God Has Planted You* (Ventura, CA: Regal Books, 1994), 241.

[100] Bobby Clinton, *The Making of a Leader* (Colorado Springs, CO: NavPress, 1988), 131.

things like guiding in a reading programme. Since readers make leaders there are few more influential ways to impact young lives than to get them reading the books and articles that have changed your life! You should have something extraordinary to offer them, then, be it expertise in a field, or success in an area of ministry they are aspiring to, or show spiritual giftedness for. Engstrom, in this regard, says, 'If a mentor is not stretching his protégé, he does not have mentoring relationship'.[101] Along these lines, I have started a Book Club in our church. The same small group reads the same book and we meet every other month to discuss its impact on our thinking and lives. It is actually a way I can convey my philosophy of ministry in an informal way, especially since the group wants the majority of the books selected to be from a list of books most influential on me.

Mentoring as well as modelling can be treated to a large extent as the ministry-of-killing-two-birds-with-one-stone. While exclusive one-to-one sessions are essential to good mentoring (Longenecker suggests meeting every other week as a goal for pastors to mentor congregation members[102]), 'the mark of a mentoring pastor is his habit of having other men beside him [in ministry] whenever possible.'[103] Quality leaders in the making require quality time being groomed for their future roles.

Such a one-on-one pattern in leadership training is found throughout Scripture. One of the most striking examples is Moses' mentoring of Joshua. Naomi taught Ruth. Elijah prepared Elisha. Paul groomed Timothy. Peter worked with Mark. The list goes on and on. Mentoring will be a significant ministry of those who aspire to be servant leaders.

---

[101] Ted Engstrom, *The Fine Art of Mentoring*, 77.
[102] Harold Longenecker, *Growing Leaders by Design*, 153.
[103] Ibid., 154.

Conclusion

Accessibility is expressed in many different ways – as we have shown in this chapter. In reviewing this chapter some months after I wrote the first draft, I realized that whether we are talking about modelling or mentoring, a very practical way to lead in these directions has been left out. One of the best ways that people can learn from you as a leader is to invite them into your home to spend time with them over a meal. Hospitality is an increasingly missing virtue in the evangelical church in the west; we have opted for making our homes virtual fortresses, cocooning ourselves so as to escape the pressures of contemporary life. In a similar vein Winzenburg maintains, 'Cellular phones and the Internet make us feel comfortable with electronic relationships while avoiding the flesh-and-blood people in need around us.'[104] Yet hospitality is not listed as a gift of the Spirit so much as it is an obligation for every believer. Thus Romans 12:13 declares quite bluntly: 'Practise hospitality.' Hebrews 13:2 says, 'Do not forget to entertain strangers.' Gaius is exalted as an exemplary elder in 3 John 5 because of his lifestyle of providing hospitality in the church. One of the qualifications for eldership in 1 Timothy 3:2 and Titus 1:8 is 'being given to hospitality'. Our family ended up sticking with the first church we visited when we moved to Port Colborne some years ago because a family there invited us home for lunch after the morning service the first Sunday we attended the church. Yes, providing hospitality is costly and so that is why it is a by-product of servanthood.

---

[104] Stephen Winzenburg, 'Whatever Happened To Hospitality?', *Christianity Today* (May 22, 2000), 79.

4

Affability: It's a team sport

The dictionary defines *affable* as 'pleasant and easy to approach or talk to; friendly'. Now why would this be such an important quality in a servant leader? After all, did not Casey Stengel, the celebrated New York Yankee baseball manager, not without reason, coin that famous expression, 'Nice guys finish last!'? Well, if you cannot see people as being the heart of your ministry, you have missed something pretty fundamental about Christian leadership. If you cannot get along with people, then you are disqualified as a servant leader. One of the characteristics that you can tie(*ty*)-in to servant leadership in every case is this uncanny ability to put people first in service. It means being at home with people. Viv Thomas captures this quality nicely when describing the leader of the future: 'I do not think it is an exaggeration to say that the future of the church depends on its leadership being relationally-rooted people. This will mean an ongoing conversation with their heavenly Father and a similar conversation with those whom they have been called to lead.'[105]

This principle might seem like a truism but the sad fact of the matter is that due to the excessive individualism

---

[105] Viv Thomas, *Future Leader* (Carlisle, UK: Paternoster Press, 1999), 12.

engendered in our society, and the narcissism of human nature, it is too easily found to be missing. John Wesley was on target when he stated that 'Christianity is essentially a social religion rather than a solitary religion'.[106] Of course, he proved how much he really believed in this corporate understanding of the faith by the way he formed bands and classes of small numbers of converts to ensure that they had the support and accountability he felt was necessary for individual converts' rapid spiritual growth. Christianity is a team sport, then, not one we engage in as individual competitors.

People get the results

The emphasis in secular corporations today is that people are what make the business work. Not efficiency. Not technology. Not management by objectives. Leaders increasingly see their role as being that of creating an environment whereby employees share a mission statement, vision, values, and goals that highly motivate them in their work. Gardener puts it this way: 'Wise leaders are continually finding ways to say to their constituents, "I hear you".'[107] Kanter similarly makes this observation in her classic management book, *The Change Masters*: 'The companies with reputations for progressive human resource practices were significantly higher in long term profitability and financial growth than their counterparts.'[108]

Such has not always been the case. The first half of the twentieth century was dominated by a management

---

[106] Quoted in Howard Snyder, *The Radical Wesley*, 117.
[107] John Gardener, *On Leadership*, 27.
[108] Rosabeth Moss Kanter, *The Change Masters*, 19.

school of thought that looked on employees as means to an end, resulting in authoritarian leadership. People were viewed as machines or instruments to be manipulated by their leaders for organizational ends. People-oriented as opposed to task-oriented theory dominated the last half century, however. The leader's function increasingly became that of facilitating employee co-operation and attainment, with human resources being perceived as the most valuable asset of the company. A more democratic style of leadership was thus nurtured. Communication flowed more vertically, as well as continuing to flow horizontally. Workers shared in developing rewards, improving working conditions, and appraising progress toward goals, or even in helping set corporate goals. Hence Peters and Waterman could make the observation that 'the companies with reputations for progressive human resource practices were significantly higher in long-term profitability and financial growth than their counterparts'.[109] According to a recent report of the American Management Association, an overwhelming majority of the two hundred managers polled in a survey agreed that the single most important skill of an executive was his or her ability to get along with people.

Nevertheless, when you put your ear to the ground, you discover that it is still largely a dog eat dog world! The corporate hierarchy still exists. People-serving and friendly bosses are still as common as spotted zebras. Look no further than the fallen nature of the human race to give a partial answer to this lack of people-first servant leadership. We should not be surprised, then, at Kanter's list of attitudes that sabotage effective use of people and therefore of more productivity.

---

[109] Thomas Peters and Robert Waterman, *In Search of Excellence*, 19.

- Regard any new idea from below with suspicion.
- Ask departments or individuals to challenge each other's proposals.
- Insist that people who need your approval to act first go through several levels of management to get their signatures.
- Express your criticisms freely and withhold your praise.
- Control everything carefully.
- Spring changes on people unexpectedly to keep them on their toes.
- Don't give out information too freely.
- Don't forget that as their boss you automatically know everything important about the business.[110]

There seems to be a meeting of minds in current thinking about leadership from both secular and Christian sources. It revolves around a theory called a systems approach to management. Stephen Covey urges companies to develop this holistic approach to running businesses resulting, in his opinion, in a win-win venture whereby company objectives and employee well-being can be simultaneously achieved – instead of being pitted constantly against each other.[111] Similarly, in *Management for Your Church*, Lindgren and Shawchuck contend that a *systems* way of running an organization is the way of the future: it merges *traditional* (task-oriented) and *human* (people-oriented) approaches, seeing them as having equal merit.

How does the systems approach stack up biblically? It might well be argued that it is a theologically-justified concept. Repeatedly in Scripture, a fine balance seems to be striven for in urging the denial of self in the cross-carrying activity of kingdom-building (Mark 10:30),

---

[110] Rosabeth Moss Kanter, *The Change Masters*, 101.

[111] Stephen Covey, *Principle-Centered Leadership*, 192.

and yet holding the promise of a new life in Christ which is personally enriching and which requires careful stewarding (John 10:10). God is both in the business of enlisting us for his royal service in a demanding and sacrificial way (hence the task orientation of the parable of the talents), and in investing our lives with meaning (hence the character formation stated as being a primary goal for God's people in Romans 8:28,29). Jesus gave specific and kingdom-targeting work to the disciples to do when he sent them out two by two, but that work was not given impersonally: he interfaced with them at each step of their training and service (Luke 10). Healthy churches are those which are outward looking (focus on evangelism of the lost: task-orientation) and inward looking (focus on edification of the saints: people-orientation) simultaneously. Churches become dysfunctional when they fall into the trap of stressing one at the expense of the other. God's people need to be seated and sent in an ongoing rhythm, like waves ebbing and flowing at the seashore. In a similar vein, summarizing their theory of a systems approach to leadership, Lindgren and Shawchuck say, 'properly understood, a systems approach to church [leadership] emphasizes the interrelationship of the prophetic (mission) and priestly (personal) roles with the kingly (managerial) role'.[112]

The time has come to recognize that people make results, and that people are the results, when it comes to fulfilling the mission of the church! John Stott says it well: 'People must take precedence over projects. And people must be neither "manipulated" nor even "managed". Though the latter is less demeaning than the former, both words are derived from *manus*, meaning

---

[112] Alvin Lindgren and Norman Shawchuck, *Management For Your Church*, 137–138.

hand, and expressing a "handling" of people as if they were commodities rather than persons.'[113] In a word, sergetting the job done and meeting the needs of your people at the same time. Remarkably, this is the big idea that has increasingly gripped secular management thinking, as witnessed for example, in addition to Covey's popularity, in the writing and teaching of Robert Greenleaf. He pleads that, in the final analysis, leadership, to be effective, must be about service, and so styles his preferred leader as a *servant*, quite a remarkable admission by a non-biblicist.[114]

So what does this 'high touch' style of leadership look like then? What are its attitudes and behaviours? In what ways does affability evidence servant leadership? In this chapter, we will see that affability reveals the face of listening well, fostering team work, affirming others, and mastering the art of delegation.

Listening well

There is no question in my mind that the leadership skill most lacking in my skill-set, especially in the early years, has been listening well. Even when I did appear to be listening intently to someone, I must confess that I was quiet more often because I was busy formulating in my own mind how I was going to answer the person talking than I was absorbed in seeking understanding. It took getting married and having my wife retort, 'You're not listening', to get me in touch with the fact that I had

---

[113] John Stott, 'What Makes Leadership Christian?', *Christianity Today* (August 9, 1985), 26.
[114] Robert K. Greenleaf, *The Power of Servant Leadership* Larry C. Spears (ed.), (San Francisco: Berrett-Koehler, 1998), X.

developed the art of appearing interested and involved in a conversation when I was not. Bonhoeffer must have had me in mind when he wrote: 'There is a kind of listening with half an ear that presumes already to know what the other person has to say. It is an impatient, inattentive listening, that despises the brother and is only waiting for a chance to speak and thus get rid of the other person. This is no fulfillment of our obligation, and is certain that here too our attitude to our brother only reflects our relationship to God.'[115]

In spite of the pride leaders take in knowing the art of communicating well, they seem to forget that there is more to communication than talk; listening is an important aspect of effective two-way connecting. Nevertheless, leaders specialize in pontificating. Many organizational and relational problems stem from a failure to recognize the two-way nature of communication. It is well-established that approximately only 10 per cent of communication is through words, with 30 per cent represented by our sounds or tones, and 60 per cent by our body language.

What does listening have to do with servant leadership? Stephen Covey expresses the correlation well: 'Empathetic listening is . . . risky. It takes a great deal of security to go into a deep listening experience because you open yourself up to be influenced. You become vulnerable. It's a paradox, in a sense, because in order to have influence, you have to be influenced.'[116] This insight is seen no more obviously expressed, in my exposure to various leaders, than with Joseph D'Souza, currently CEO of Operation Mobilisation in India. Joseph has the uncanny knack of

---

[115] Dietrich Bonhoeffer, *Life Together* (New York: Harper & Row, 1954), 98.

[116] Stephen Covey, *Principle-Centered Leadership*, 243.

giving his undivided and empathetic attention to whoever is conversing with him. Although it is not easy to get
quality time alone with him (after all he is leader of seven
hundred national missionaries), what is lacking in
quantity is made up in quality. His flair for listening well
partially explains the loyalty he elicits from his co-
workers. He is a fulfilment of what Covey had in mind
when he wrote, 'Real listening shows respect. It creates
trust. As we listen, we not only gain understanding; we
also create the environment to be understood.'[117]

There is nothing that disarms people and wins them
over to your point of view as much as their sensing that
you have heard them out first. When I took counselling
courses as part of my theological preparation for the
pastoral ministry, I will never forget my professor commenting that the most essential quality in a counsellor
was to be a good listener because ultimately most people
had the solutions to their own struggles, and simply needed
someone who would provide them with the opportunity to
verbalize their deep-set intuition. Is this not what Proverbs
20:5 has in mind in maintaining that 'the purposes of a
man's heart are deep waters, but a man of understanding
draws them out'? Especially with pastors, listening well is
indispensable to shepherding effectively. Watchman Nee
lists listening well as an indispensable quality of the
Christian leader.[118]

Again, Stephen Covey is articulate in the way he talks to
management about building up what he calls 'emotional
dividends' with colleagues and co-workers through becoming good listeners. He says, 'Seek first to understand, then
to be understood. This principle is the key to effective

[117] Ibid., 214.
[118] Watchman Nee, *The Normal Christian Worker* (Bombay: Gospel
Literature Service, *sic*.), 31–39.

interpersonal communication'.[119] According to Peters and Waterman, 'the excellent companies are better listeners'.[120] Conversely, it could be argued that companies that do not foster good listening in their organizational culture do not do well in business. Backing that assertion up, one study found that sixty per cent of misunderstandings in business is due to poor listening, that eight per cent of all business communication has to be repeated, and that eighty per cent of our day is spent in communication of one form or another.[121] Speaking of Christian ministries, Viv Thomas makes an astonishing but probably prophetic observation that much of the disunity they face may be traced back to an unwillingness to listen well to one another.[122]

There are ways to grow in an ability to listen well. For instance, look the talker in the eye. If someone has an appointment with you in your office, do not shuffle papers while the other person is talking. Also, instruct your secretary not to forward calls to you while you are in a formal appointment. Turn off your cell phone. After all, the telephone caller has not spent a half hour getting to your office like your visitor may have.

At its heart, listening well to fellow human beings is symptomatic of a genuine spirituality. True, it can also be a function of personality; some people by nature or nurture are more relational. However, just as love can be described as a feeling to be learned, so listening empathetically can be learned. Failure to acquire this skill as a

---

[119] Ibid., 237.

[120] Thomas Peters and Robert Waterman, *In Search of Excellence*, 193.

[121] Kenneth Blanchard, 'Listening: A Basic Business Survival Skill', *Inside Guide* (June/July 1992), 12.

[122] Viv Thomas, *Future Leader*, 38.

leader indicts us as likely being the type not to make time to listen to God either. As Bonhoeffer puts it: 'He who can no longer listen to his brother will soon be no longer listening to God either; he will be doing nothing but prattle in the presence of God too.'[123]

Or, to articulate the principle positively: 'To listen to others quiets and disciplines the mind to listen to God . . . When we grow dull in listening to God we would do well to listen to others in silence and see if we do not hear God.'[124]

As I pen these words, I have just spent, the evening before, four hours in back-to-back counselling sessions – not all of which were planned. In most of those sessions, I could not help realizing that I did a lot of listening. Eugene Peterson, speaking as a pastor, observes this: 'Listening is in such short supply in the world today; people aren't used to being listened to . . . Pastoral listening requires unhurried leisure, even if it's only for five minutes . . . Speaking to people does not have the same personal intensity as listening to them.'[125] May God help us leaders to perceive that listening to others is at the heart of servanthood and that it is a reflection of affability, that is, of the love for people that is at the heart of true ministry.

Team work

When Roger Smith took over as the CEO of General Motors, the world's biggest car manufacturer, he took his

---

[123] Dietrich Bonhoeffer, *Life Together*, 98.

[124] Richard Foster, *Celebration of Discipline* (Sevenoaks, UK: Hodder and Stoughton, 1984), 121.

[125] Eugene Peterson, *The Contemplative Pastor* (Grand Rapids, MI: W.B. Eerdmans, 1993), 21.

top five hundred executives on a five day retreat to learn from them and to share his vision for the company. He followed the example of a predecessor, Alfred Sloan, who demonstrated his valuing of team leadership by taking three days every quarter to mull over the career path of his top one thousand executives person by person. To him, making GM a success was not a solo effort.

We get a glimpse of affability in a leader when we see that he or she is at ease in working with a team. Already we have reviewed how Jesus and Paul worked hand in glove with people as the key strategy to getting their work done. In the history of Protestantism, in spite of the Reformation's rediscovery of the biblical concept of the priesthood of all believers, the church, for the most part, has been led by a professional elite. Whether intentionally or not, the translators of the *Authorized Version* introduced a comma into Ephesians 4:12, which reinforced the misconception that ordained pastors were to do most of the ministry in the local church.[126] Pastors and teachers, according to this text, are to 'prepare God's people for works of service'. Interjecting a comma after 'people' implies that the pastors and teachers are to do the work of service. Instead, the emphasis should be on pastors and teachers equipping the whole church, so that every member, gifted by the Spirit in different ways for mutual upbuilding, does the actual work. Indeed, team work is the God-ordained way to do ministry. It may not always be as neat and tidy as doing it yourself, but over the long haul it is the group effort that will be the most enriching, that is, the most effective (Eph. 4:16).

A team-first style of leadership has been compared to conducting a jazz band. The difference between

---

[126] Paul Stevens, *Liberating the Laity* (Downer's Grove, IL: InterVarsity, 1985), 14.

conducting a jazz band and an orchestra is considerable. The conductor of an orchestra requires all the musicians to follow his or her lead precisely. There is no toleration of deviation or of prima donnas. The interpretation of the music becomes the conductor's prerogative. On the other hand, the conductor of the jazz band encourages all members to let their personalities shine through. The best in each musician is drawn out. A creative synergy is produced which is not limited by the musical score, even though the basic tune must be followed. Attention thus centres on the musicians themselves rather than the conductor.[127]

The synergy of teams can be seen in different ways. Even a team approach to overall leadership has great potential. Numerous examples, such as George Wilson teaming successfully with Billy Graham to run their massive evangelistic organization, are cited in a fascinating article called 'Should the CEO Be One Person?' in the *World Executive's Digest* of February 1993. Looking back over three decades of observing various styles of leadership in Christian ministries, there have been several illustrations that come to my mind of effective leadership teams. In India in the 1970s and early eighties, Alfy Franks and Ray Eicher were co-executives of OM-India. They had separate areas of responsibility and yet consulted one another on major issues before a decision was made by the one whose purview it fell under. Their different personalities and strengths meshed well and enabled OM there to weather its turbulent 'teen' years. Alfy was the gentle, people-oriented pastor-type and Ray was the prophetic visionary. Similarly, George Verwer

---

[127] Max DePree, 'Leadership Jazz', J. Thomas Wren (ed.), *The Leader's Companion: Insights On Leadership Through the Ages* (New York: The Free Press, 1995), 453.

and Peter Maiden have worked effectively as a team. Even though very different in temperament, they have always supported one another loyally and given each other the benefit of the doubt publicly. George is the visionary and Peter the manager. Together they have run OM well for two decades and will be sorely missed as a team when a change in overall leadership comes in September 2003.

Teams. Whether they be leadership teams or work teams led by one person, one cannot help observing that most great leaders in church history were not lone ranger leaders. Leaders as diverse as the North African theologian, Augustine, and the father of modern missions, William Carey, while prodigious in their individual accomplishments, nevertheless insisted on functioning in ministry through teams. Just stopping for a moment to focus on one of these, William Carey, we would be remiss to overlook his close colleagues in trying to define the reasons for his singular success in translating the Bible into forty South Asian languages at a time when the Bible had been rendered in only twenty non-European languages by 1800.[128] It was not only the Serampore Trio who were instrumental in the array of evangelistic and social accomplishments associated with William Carey, but Carey knew how to attract and surround himself with a team of savvy technicians and learned scholars from various parts of India.[129] Such giants of church history, then, have had the discernment to know that certain steps in spiritual growth could occur best in a group setting or that certain ministry

---

[128] Sunil Chatterjee, 'Memoirs of Serampore Translations', *Dharma Deepika* (June 1999), 59.
[129] This team approach to Carey's ministry is well-documented in ibid., 59–66.

breakthroughs could not be accomplished alone. Martin
Luther had his table talk companions. John Wesley had
his methodical growth cells. Moody had his Sankey.

Little wonder that there is renewed interest in small
groups in local churches as a key to growth. The remarkable house church movement in Great Britain is a
testimony to this principle. As Longenecker maintains,
'Certain key growth steps are more likely to occur in
groups than in one-to-one interactions . . . It is only in the
community of faith that we can become whole persons,
learning to accept ourselves and extend acceptance to
others.'[130] One of the forerunners of this rediscovery of
the corporate nature not only of ministry but of growth
in the church has been Larry Richards. Hear him in *A
New Face for the Church*

> In our culture, large meetings of the congregation draw men
> and women together who seldom see each other during the
> week. They do not truly *know* each other. They can not truly
> love, because they are not involved in each other's lives. In a
> larger congregation most of us remain strangers. Few have
> opportunity to share themselves. Few would feel free to be
> truly honest. The Bible suggests that Christians should even
> "get into the habit of admitting their sins to one another, and
> praying for one another" (James 5:13). How many of us trust
> the larger congregation to the extent that we would admit our
> sins – and if we did, how many in that congregation would
> pray, and how many would gossip? . . . To learn to trust, and
> to become trustworthy . . . a church is forced to move to a
> small group structure.
>
>   . . . The church is a *transforming* community, it is not a
> *transformed* one. It is made up, not of perfect people, but of
> sinners who are struggling to experience the life of God that

---

[130] Harold Longenecker, *Growing Leaders by Design*, 33.

is within them. Our acceptance by God is not based upon our perfection. God knows us and loves us and receives us *as we are.* So we must learn to accept, and love, *imperfect* people in the church – including ourselves! As we learn to be honest with ourselves and with each other, God can deal with our sins and our imperfections. He can transform us. But for this to happen we must open ourselves up to God and to others in the church . . .

As a [small] group is constructed with a high level of trust, individuals are able to lower their defenses and develop satisfying relationships with others. They become freer in expressing and accepting their caring feelings. Because it satisfies and rewards the individual, each venture toward accepting the reaction of others and expressing helpful feelings toward others reinforces the next venture. As a group grows in its capacity to support [one another], risk taking becomes easier.[131]

Small groups (one form of teams) in the local church context, then, can be instrumental in spiritual growth, and it is a wise pastor who seizes the day in facilitating small group ministry in a church for this reason. Servant leaders don't have to micro-manage things: you can't when you lead through teams or small groups because there are a lot of loose ends, but they do maximize productivity. Small groups that start out as driven by the need to foster enriching fellowship often end up as outlets for doing ministry together. One need not form a small group or team just to get certain projects done for often as fellowship or study groups mature they discover the multiplicity of gifts in their midst that can be put to good use for the sake of the kingdom.

---

[131] Larry Richards, *A New Face for the Church* (Grand Rapids, MI: Zondervan, 1981), 153, 160, 161, 165.

Working through teams has the added spiritual benefit of forcing the leader to become more dependent on the Holy Spirit. This is the thesis of Howell's article concerning the apostle Paul's wonderful capacity to work through teams as he travelled around the Mediterranean world. In this regard Howell states: 'Paul's deep commitment to *team ministry* is another expression of his confidence in the Spirit. One of the keys to the success of Paul's mission was his ability to attract capable and dedicated men and women to work alongside him both in itinerant evangelism and in settled discipleship and follow up.'[132]

One further application of the importance of being team-oriented in leadership as evidence of the trait of affability, which is characteristic of servant leadership, concerns functioning in an international missions' context. As promised in the Introduction, I am seeking to illustrate how servant leadership works in the several ministry arenas of pastoring, executive leadership of organizations, and missions. As the task of proclaiming the gospel to the unreached frontiers is owned by the global church, with an increasing number of missionaries coming from the two-thirds world, there will be a more urgent pressure to personalize and de-bureaucratize international mission agencies. Small ministry units (teams) will need relative autonomy to adjust to rapidly changing circumstances in a hostile 10/40 Window environment. Moreover, many of the people on these teams will not be from the traditional sending countries but from such places as Brazil, Nigeria, Korea, and India. And these people are much

---

[132] Don N. Howell, 'Confidence in the Spirit as the Governing Ethos of the Pauline Mission', in C. Douglas McConnell (ed.), *The Holy Spirit and Mission Dynamics* (Pasadena, CA: William Carey Library, 1997), 58.

more relational than their western world counterparts.[133] Describing the sort of leader needed for this context, missionary statesman and two-thirds world missiologist Samuel Escobar astutely comments: 'Leadership teams accomplish more and better when there is a warm and deep person to person relationship as the basis for the common work. In this sense, fellowship is interrelated with mission, relationship precedes function, friendship precedes efficiency.'[134]

Summarizing well the value of doing ministry through teams as a leader, Gangel says this: 'Even the recognition of accountability only to God is a corrupt view of Christian leadership. We stand mutually accountable to each other, even to subordinates. Commitment to team ministry can deliver the leader from individualism, isolation, empire-building, and burnout.'[135]

Affirming others

Someone has cutely remarked that the tongue is the only tool that gets sharper with constant use! So it is that a leader's words can make or break a follower. That old wives' tale that 'sticks and stones can break my bones but words can never harm me' just is not true! People spend their whole lives getting over the cruel put-downs of their parents in childhood. Affirmation is like contraband

[133] For a detailed development of this argument see my book *We Are the World: Globalisation and the Changing Face of Missions* (Carlisle, UK: OM Publishing, 1999).

[134] Samuel Escobar, 'The Internationalization of Missions and Leadership Style', speech given to the EFMA Convention of 1991.

[135] Kenneth Gangel, *Feeding and Leading*, 60.

alcohol was in the Prohibition, hard to find. Leaders who have the habit of affirming those who work for them are demonstrating the affability that wins the loyalty of those around them. Affirming leaders are servant leaders. They practise what Proverbs 12:25 talks about: 'An anxious heart weighs a man down, but a kind word cheers him up.'

Even though Jesus could offer biting criticism to the religious status quo, and pointedly rebuke his disciples, he excelled at affirming his followers.[136] Before his disciples had even begun their work with him, he told them they would become fishers of men; he foresaw a glorious future ministry for them, and was not afraid to let them know that from the outset. He commended Peter for his spiritual insight (Matthew 16:17). He disarmingly called them his friends (John 15:15). He publicly promised rewards for their faithful service (Luke 22:28–30). Jesus' love for people led him to be very positive with them (see also 1 Cor. 13:6–7).

Conversely, I'm sure we've all had the type of boss who is a kill-joy. Always looking over your shoulder, Mr Kill-Joy insists that every problem and every detail be explained to him. He is the micro-manager *par excellence*. Rarely would he allow you independence to exercise your own judgment and frequently second-guesses your decisions. Making you quite aware of the one per cent you don't know or failed to do correctly, he is skilled in ignoring the 99 per cent of the job that you excelled in.[137]

Affirming leadership does not view credit (affirmation) as in short supply but concludes that 'your being honoured does not reduce proportionately the amount of praise that

---

[136] P.T. Chandapilla, *The Master Trainer*, 46–53.

[137] Ian McGugan, 'The Five Worst Types of Bosses', *Small Business* (November 1989), 44.

might be forthcoming to me'. There is something empow-
ering about praising someone else's work. I guess that's
why some leaders hesitate to give it. Affirmation increases a
person's productivity because as self-confidence increases
so does productivity. Energy is not wasted in worrying
about the quality of one's work as perceived by others
when one is feeling good about one's contribution. Along
the same lines, Kirkpatrick and Locke insist that 'effective
leaders give power to others as a means of increasing their
own power.' They then go on to say, 'Effective leaders do
not see power as something that is competed for but rather
as something that can be created and distributed to
followers without detracting from their own power.'[138] The
pie can be made bigger before you divide it up: you do not
have to cut the pie up into smaller and smaller pieces!

Companies like 3M, the largest employer in the USA
after GM, see exalting the employee as a win-win situation.
Through 3M's encouraging of employees to take initiatives
to invent new product ideas by letting them develop and
market the product if their idea is accepted, the company
has spawned over sixty thousand products (like the
famous Scotch Tape). Their cultivating of *intrapreneurs* is
similar to what Frank Tillapaugh describes in his best-
selling book on the church of over a decade ago, *The
Unleashing of the Church*. His strategy was always to tell
people who came to him excited about a new ministry
idea that if they really believed in it, then they could have
the privilege of leading it. This approach to triggering
new ministry had the dual effect of training new leaders,
and of keeping ministries that were not of the Holy Spirit
from being birthed. There is nothing more affirming –
especially if you have nascent leadership gifting ability

---

[138] Shelly A. Kirkpatrick and Edwin A. Locke, 'Leadership: Do Traits Matter?' in J. Thomas Wren (ed.), *The Leader's Companion*, 137.

begging for expression – than being given the chance to prove yourself! Many churches fail to grow because leadership is hoarded by the chosen few. If it is a truism that eighty per cent of the ministry in a church is done by twenty per cent of the people, it cannot also be said with authority that it is a lack of volunteers that is the heart of the problem. Too often potential workers have stopped volunteering because too many roadblocks were put in their way for meaningful involvement. Not by accident, Hans Finzel, an experienced missions' executive, identifies an absence of affirmation – which he spoofs as 'what could be better than a pay raise?' – as being one of the top ten mistakes that leaders make, in his book by that name. Affirming leaders take risks with their people. They are pleased to see the flowers around them blossom. That is why famous and successful USA college basketball coach John Wooden, when asked how he motivated his players, wise-cracked, 'I catch them doing something right.'[139]

One of the major reasons why leaders fail to give credit where credit is due is because of their dismal view of human nature. Back in 1960, a concept was proposed by Douglas MacGregor which explained why some leaders treat the group of people who work for them negatively in order to get results, while others treat their people positively. Theory Y assumes that the leader's power is granted by the group he or she leads and that human beings are basically self-starters and creative at work if positively motivated. Theory X says that the leader's power is derived from the position he or she occupies and that human beings are intrinsically lazy and unreliable and so have to be coerced into co-operation. Theory X leaders therefore lead in an authoritarian way and are

---

[139] Quoted in Calvin Miller, *Leadership*, 62.

task-oriented. Theory Y leaders are democratic in style and are people-oriented.[140] Obviously we have all experienced both types of leaders and the affirming leader is the Theory Y leader.

Interestingly enough, church growth consultant, Kenon Callaghan, concurs with what is being proffered here. He argues that Theory Y leadership is preferable in training organizations like the church because it enables such organizations to be this way:

- '*Proactive:* A strong sense of self-directed, self-initiated action, with power and authority, exists in the grouping.
- *Relational:* There is a genuine spirit of compassion in the grouping.
- *Missional:* A solid sense exists of common, shared meanings as to the purpose of life.
- *Intentional:* There is a high level of creativity and hope.'[141]

The art of delegation

Former President of World Vision, Ted Engstrom, claims that delegation is the single most important skill that can be acquired by the Christian executive.[142] Again, Hans Finzel lists the lack of delegation as being in his list of top ten mistakes leaders make. I must confess that early on in my leadership I was known as someone who tried to do almost everything myself. The folly of that attitude and behaviour became quite clear through an unfortunate

---

[140] Paul Hershey and Ken Blanchard, *Management of Organizational Behavior*, 59–62.

[141] Kenon Callaghan, *Effective Church Leadership*, 148.

[142] Ted Engstrom, *The Making of a Christian Leader* (Grand Rapids, MI: Zondervan, 1976).

accident in 1974. I was serving with OM in India and had been given the responsibility of organizing a massive evangelistic programme in the largest state, Uttar Pradesh. I had mapped out a detailed outreach in 48 different districts involving 25 teams and 250 people for three months. Not only that but I also drove one of the evangelism vehicles, five-ton British lorries, with which evangelism teams of primarily nationals were taken around to different villages and bazaars, to do their open air preaching and tract distribution.

I remember leaving our training conference in Lucknow in my heart priding myself at being so indispensable. I had just finished smoothly administrating this large conference and here I was now driving a truck, knowing drivers were at a premium (only foreigners were allowed to drive these foreign vehicles). Barely had I thought these vain thoughts when I heard a thump. Looking out my side view mirror, I discovered, 'horror of horrors', that I had run over someone I had not seen in the blind spot in my mirror, as I had turned onto a busy side street near the centre of the city. Those in the box (back) of the truck rushed out and quickly bundled the struck person into the back of the truck so that we could hustle off to the hospital before a mob developed and attacked me (the driver is usually assumed to be at fault in India and it is not unknown for drivers in accidents to be severely beaten or even killed, even if the accident is not their fault). But my comrades could not carry the victim off the street until I had first moved forward slightly. You see, as soon as I had heard the thump, I braked. The only thing was that I braked right on top of the foot of this villager, who then fell over backwards, foot still pinned under the wheel. When the man was bundled into the back of the truck, my friends discovered that the foot was only hanging on by the front tendons. I remember driving to the hospital and thinking, 'Lord, have mercy on me for being so proud as to think I was indispensable'. I knew in my heart of hearts that the Lord was teaching me a lesson here. I was being reminded in a costly way that God does not need any one of us to accomplish his purposes. Let him receive the glory.

In fact the story of the Bible is the story of a creative and sovereign God who specializes in Plan B because he can't always use his first choice to do his will and accomplish his purposes. Theologians thus distinguish between the perfect and the permissive will of God. A biblical illustration of this principle at work is King Saul being set aside and a shepherd boy exalted as king in his place.

Anyhow, you might want to know what happened to that accident victim. He was from one of the surrounding villages, a Hindu man. Sorry to say, he lost his foot, but he did accept Jesus Christ as his Saviour. All things worked together for good.

Yes, learning to delegate is what I should have taken pride in. Generally, much more can be accomplished through a group than one person. We considered that to some extent in the last chapter in our consideration of the importance of team work. That is why D.L. Moody was known to have frequently wise-cracked that 'I'd rather get ten men to do the job than for me to do the job of ten men'. Delegation can take different forms. George Verwer has always had someone different serve with him as a practical worker and errand runner every year. That person is called a gopher, someone who 'goes for this and goes for that'. Such people are needed: they often enjoy doing menial or manual jobs because they have the spiritual gift of helps. For example, my wife finds it very rewarding to stuff envelopes for two hours at a time – a chore we had to do frequently over the years as we sent missionary prayer letters to our many prayer partners. Needless to say, along with her two other discernible spiritual gifts, she has the gift of helps.

An astute leader 'reads' his or her people well enough to assign different types of tasks or roles to different types of team members. In his fascinating story of leading Service Masters in the USA, evangelical executive, William Pollard, makes much the same point when he talks about his success in mobilizing people: 'Build your team of people around the talents and skills of the ordinary person, not just around the skills and talents of those few extraordinary people.'[143]

If delegation is so wonderful, why don't more leaders demonstrate skill at delegating? Here's an incomplete list of reasons.

- Fear of losing authority
- Fear that the job won't be done as well as you can do it
- Fear of work being done better
- Fear that it will take too long to train the other person
- Poor role models of delegation in the past by your leaders
- Fear of dependency on others developing

One of the least understood benefits of being a delegating leader is that it is an effective tool in training leaders. When a team member is given responsibility and the freedom to do the job his or her own way (within reason), it allows that person to demonstrate their capacity to handle pressure, relate to other people, complete assignments, take initiative, handle criticism, and be industrious, among other things. As church growth expert Callaghan observes: 'People learn leadership best in an environment wherein there is a high delegation of authority, not

---

[143] William C. Pollard, *The Soul of the Firm* (Grand Rapids, MI: Zondervan, 1996), 147.

responsibilities . . . The more fully persons are given authority, the more likely they are to develop their leadership competencies.'[144] Covey refers to having input into future leaders' lives through foresightful delegation as 'leaving a legacy'. He furthermore identifies this as 'stewardship delegation', that is, the more hands-off kind that enables participants to feel that they are active participants in the process of getting the job done.[145]

Delegating without micro-managing has another redeeming feature.[146] It recognizes and releases the multi-gifted laity, viewing them as the key to ministry and to do the bulk of the ministry in the local church. Church leaders, especially pastors, need to jealously defend the faith against false doctrine, but not the pulpit! Paul Stevens puts it this way: 'The notion that one person could so embody the charismatic gifts of ministry for the church he or she might be called the minister is not only a practical heresy. It is an affront to the head Equipper.'[147] Ministry opportunities should not be hoarded, like some stockpile of nuclear weapons, nor should they be overseen heavy-handedly – as if the Holy Spirit cannot lead all believers or as if there is not a supernatural head of the church, the Lord Jesus Christ. In other words, the foot has as much connection to the head as does the hand

---

[144] Kenon Callaghan, *Effective Church Leadership*, 154.

[145] Stephen Covey, *First Things First* (New York: Fireside, 1991), 224.

[146] While delegating should not be done in such a way that the leader is always looking over the shoulder of the one to whom the job has been given, neither should a strictly *laissez-faire* approach be taken. People should be followed up on to make sure they understand the task assigned and to hold them accountable to meet deadlines.

[147] Paul Stevens, *Liberating the Laity*, 36.

(1 Cor. 12). Christ is our Head and so leaders should walk softly in deference to the true Leader.

That is not to say that leaders and pastors should not train, and work with, those released into ministry. We've already established the importance of equipping. Beck and Yeager maintain in their book on how the four basic leadership styles can be put to work effectively that the best kind of leadership is that which delegates readily and yet is available for support when subordinates need assistance.[148] In feedback from employees in various companies they come to this conclusion:

> To do their best work, people want you to give them complete information, including directions, advice, explanations, and consequences . . .Then they want you to trust them, delegate meaningful responsibilities to them, give them the authority they need to do what you hired them to do . . . When they get stuck, as everyone does sooner or later, they want your support to help them think through their own decisions without undercutting their sense of responsibility . . . And finally, if they are stuck, and need you to step up to the plate, they want you to listen to their ideas and make timely decisions based on their recommendations.[149]

Conclusion

Thinking once again about the example of Christ, we can quickly determine that he was a master delegator. He gave his disciples a variety of assignments whether that

---

[148] John D.W. Beck and Neil M. Yeager, *The Leader's Window*, 153.
[149] Ibid., 155–156.

be feeding the five thousand on the one hand, or casting out demons, on the other. The Twelve had to provide a treasurer, find a donkey, prepare a dining room, and preach the kingdom of God. No task was too menial nor too spiritual for them to do. All this was done with careful supervision but also with trust.[150] At its root, we could call such delegation empowerment. That is what Miller had in mind in this statement: 'As others [through your delegation] feel more responsible for your work, they begin to care about the outcome. But in order to build a true team spirit, you must delegate accountability and glory as well as responsibility.'[151] Empowerment, then, is what results from affability. Affability is that serving quality that stems from a love for people. It is a trait of affection that is displayed by being sold on doing ministry through teams, being quick to make others look good, having a capacity to listen well, and of taking risks with others by delegating willingly.

In some African languages there is no word for cousin. The children of one's parents' sisters and brothers are your sisters and brothers. In the extended family, every cousin then would call you mom or dad![152] That should be our attitude as we work together in the body of Christ. When we reach the point, already found in the church in the two-thirds world, of experiencing self-identity in terms of the community, our individualism will have withered sufficiently to enable us to be the genuine servant leaders who demonstrate affability because we love the very people who define who we are.

---

[150] Chandapilla, *The Master Trainer*, 40–44.
[151] Calvin Miller, *Leadership*, 79.
[152] Gottfried Osei-Mensah, *Wanted: Servant Leaders* (Accra, Ghana: Africa Christian Press, 1990), 65.

Vulnerability: Leading from a position of weakness

One of the temptations of leadership is always to want to cast oneself in a good light. And leaders certainly have the means to orchestrate good public relations for themselves. We have already talked about the centrality of transparency among servant leaders. Let's now develop that theme further, in effect, expanding on what true humility is as it is practised among leaders. As has so often been the case thus far, I cannot help referencing George Verwer's example. He refuses to allow a biography to be written about him, for a long time not even permitting his photo to be published in any magazine or publicity of OM, so the few snippets mentioned herein will surely find a fascinated audience! What I have been constantly astounded by over the years is his uncanny ability to poke fun at himself. His self-deprecating humour is not a communication technique (although it functions as such) but evidence of a real vulnerability borne out of an insightful discernment of his own fallenness, and therefore of the grace of God. Whether it be to admit publicly to having sexual temptations, confessing to his trigger-happy temper, or musing about his proneness to despair at times, we ironically come away admiring him all the more. It surely takes a person of sterling character not to hide personal weakness in an attempt to encourage fellow strugglers. To allow oneself to be vulnerable in this way reveals a generos*ity* and vulnerabil*ity* of spirit which is tied *(tyd)* to what it means to be a servant leader.

In expositing the path of servanthood taken by the Son of God in taking on human form in Philippians 2, the earthly expression of that serving mindset is fleshed out in the first five verses. Verse three is particularly apropos here for it implies a self-effacing for the sake of those around oneself: 'Do nothing out of selfish ambition or vain conceit, but in humility consider others better than yourselves.' This concern for others' welfare is elaborated on in the next verse, then: 'Each of you should look not only to your own interests, but also to the interests of others.' This passage is not trying to make the servant leader into some sort of a super-spiritual nerd. We need to pay attention to our own interests: we just do not stop there. This generosity and vulnerability of spirit, that is not self-absorbed, is usually triggered by not holding on to power so tightly that we have to defend a reputation or project an aura of invincible strength. Instead we lead from a position of weakness. It is manifested in several ways: not sacrificing long-term goals for short-term gain, allowing co-workers the freedom to make mistakes, admitting weaknesses and being open to criticism, trusting others to lead in your absence, planning for your successor, accepting the burden of higher expectations placed on you, and accepting that it is lonely at the top. It is an example of grace made perfect in weakness.

Committed to long-term gain over short-term pain

How easy it is to go with the flow – at least for now! Change is painful. The best leaders do not resist change but embrace it. As Leith Anderson wisely states: 'One thing is impossible: we cannot stay the same. We cannot stop the clock of change. If we choose to respond by doing nothing, change will take control and impose its will.'[153] I've just returned home from visiting a Christian bookstore in Toronto. There has been a change of ownership in it. The previous owner believed that you had to offer a book at full price always. As a result, he had many outdated, dog-eared, and fading books which languished unsold on the shelves. No wonder the business was nearing bankruptcy. He failed to discern the times – which in part means that the consumer is always looking for a bargain, a sale. Through these loss-leaders people will buy a larger volume of books at full value since they would not have been drawn to the shop in the first place if it were not for the advertisements about the sale. And everyone knows that most people make purchases spontaneously. The comfortable old ways of doing things just do not cut it much of the time. Of course, I am not advocating that one compromise biblical morality, where that is clear-cut. But new wine must be placed in new wineskins.

The best organizations are always going through a process of change whereby they throw out the worst and retain the best.[154] This sorting out process guarantees stability and relevance, even if it is obtained at great short-term cost and stress. It has been argued among church growth gurus, to switch organizational realms, that the

---

[153] Leith Anderson, *Dying For Change* (Minneapolis, MN: Bethany House Publishers, 1990), 140.

[154] This thesis is especially developed in Rosabeth Moss Kanter's *The Change Masters* and Peter Senge's *The Fifth Dimension: The Art and Practice of the Learning Organization* (New York: Doubleday, 1990).

churches that flourish are the ones where pastors achieve longevity.[155] Being a pastor for a long time in a church is no guarantee that a church will grow, but it seems that good pastors, if they can get past the inevitable resistance to change and the regular onslaught of the spiritual warfare faced after the initial honeymoon period wears off (often translated as conflict with difficult congregational members), will lead their churches to new heights. Short-term pain, long-term gain. That's the message. It takes an unselfish leader to think this way.

When the profit margin is temporarily put on hold, for the long-term benefits that can accrue through intensive capital investment or whatever, you are dealing with leaders who have a true serving heart: they are not worried about how things appear to their shareholders or parishioners *now* so much as they have their hearts set on reaping the long-term results *then*. An illustration of this would be a pastor who is more concerned to fill ministry positions with those who are spiritually gifted for those opportunities, and so waits for the right person to come along, or takes the time to train that person properly, versus the one who grabs the nearest warm body. It looks good on paper to have those positions filled right away but in the long run it leads to less fruitful ministry, to burnout of workers, to disillusionment of those receiving the ministry – in a word, to dysfunctionality in the local church.

That steely commitment to the results of the future is what marks the excellent leader.[156] Covey captures this

---

[155] Kenon Callaghan, *Effective Church Leadership*, 162 and Rick Warren, *The Purpose Driven Church* (Grand Rapids, MI: Zondervan, 1995), 31.

[156] Warren Bennis and Burt Nanus, *Leaders: The Strategies for Taking Charge*, 20.

quality well when he enunciates as follows: 'Leadership focuses on the top line. Management focuses on the bottom line. Leadership derives its power from values and correct principles. Management organizes resources to serve selected objectives to produce the bottom line.'[157] They are not willing to sacrifice the future welfare of the company for the expediency of immediate results. Paradoxically this will usually mean giving attention and priority to the human aspects of employees' problems and the building of close-knit work teams with high performance goals.[158] Cultivating these people strengths organizationally takes time, but it pays off in the long run.

Kingdom-minded thinking is always willing to bear the cross now so as to see eternal results yielded later on (Galatians 6:9). A biblical example of this is David's refusal, when provided with a golden opportunity to get a short-cut to the throne, to ambush and murder King Saul, who was hunting him down, as David hid in a cave near an unsuspecting King Saul (1 Sam. 24:6). A commitment to eventual results, no matter what the cost now, leads me to admire the church I moved to Toronto to pastor two years ago. Chinese Gospel Church in the heart of Chinatown and downtown Toronto has planted five churches in its forty-year existence. The downtown mother church remains relatively the same size, with approximately two hundred people in each of its Cantonese, Mandarin, and English congregations. I pastor the English congregation. It has deliberately chosen *not* to become a mega-church, instead focusing on the more effective means of reaching the unsaved and unchurched, church planting. It tithes its general income to future church planting efforts – quite

---

[157] Stephen Covey, *Principle-Centered Leadership*, 246.
[158] Paul Hershey and Kenneth Blanchard, *Management of Organizational Behavior*.

apart from pegging its commitment to world missions at over 25 per cent of the total budget. The mentality is that the downtown church is meant to be in a mode of perpetual leadership training. We expect to lose some of our best people on a regular basis so that they can spearhead fresh church planting efforts. With twenty thousand new immigrants from mainland China streaming into Canada every year, fourteen thousand of whom will settle in the Toronto area, the vision is timely. In 2000, Toronto's cosmopolitan city of 3.5 million people saw the Chinese become its largest visible minority with four hundred thousand people, surpassing the Italians for the first time.[159] That's called unselfishness borne out of a vision to build and extend the Kingdom of God.

Allowing followers to make mistakes

One of the most powerful tools of training is to give novices opportunities to serve and minister before they have it all together. Skill sets are learned on the job. Character formation requires the heat of the battle. There's no mystery to OM's successful track record in producing top-notch leaders. OMers have been thrown off the deep end as they went out on evangelism teams. Early on, OM learned the power of *learning by doing* as much as by hearing. Trial and error learning forges character. It *makes* more than *breaks* a learner. Surely that was Jesus' method in sending out the Twelve before they had completed three years of seminary and three years of language learning! It can be painful for an experienced leader to allow followers on his or her ministry team to

---

[159] Those of British ancestry historically settled Toronto and still form close to fifty per cent of the population.

bumble along. But it maps out the path of servant leadership. No doubt the ancient Chinese sage Lao-tzu had this in mind in his comment that 'true self-interest teaches selflessness . . . Enlightened leadership is service, not selfishness. The leader grows and lasts longer by placing the well-being of all above the well-being of self alone'.[160]

Successful leaders or managers know that greater productivity comes from letting those working for you have relative freedom in doing their assigned tasks their own way. In attitude, we could define this as facilitating rather than controlling.[161] Allowing people time to learn from their mistakes reflects the ways of God in fashioning our sanctification. While he has designed means of grace, like Bible reading and prayer, to mature us in Christ, requiring our proactive partnership with him, we seem to be in the habit of being sanctified as well on the basis of moving spiritually two steps forward and one step backward. Failure becomes the back door to growth! God's grace enables us to be freed to understand that he is willing and doing for his good pleasure alongside of our working out our own salvation with fear and trembling over the course of a lifetime (see Philippians 2:12,13).

Picture the process of sanctification as being similar to the growth process of the saguaro cactus. It is the most gigantic of all cacti, standing up to fifty feet tall and having as many as fifty arms. Yet the saguaro cactus has a humble beginning as a seedling which thrives best in the shadow of other desert plants, and which must be overlooked by mice, rats and weevils, which seek its succulent

---

[160] Lao-tzu, 'Tao Te Ching' in J. Thomas Wren (ed.), *The Leader's Companion*, 69.

[161] Stephen Covey, *Principle-Centered Leadership*, 190.

stems. Slowly, however, the cactus inches upward, reaching only four inches high after ten years. By the time fifty years have elapsed, the saguaro is ten feet tall: finally at seventy-five years of age it sends out its first arms.

Such patience with slow growth reckons with God's sanctification process, one which anticipates growth taking a lifetime to achieve (2 Peter 3:18; 2 Cor. 3:18). When one considers all the dysfunctionality today's generation of young people inherit from their home life – low self-esteem, sexual addiction, alcoholism, workaholism, perfectionism, and uncontrolled anger, to name just a few – all of which take considerable time to recover from normally, one should not expect instant effectiveness or maturity.[162] Leaders who are mercifully allowing their people the freedom to make mistakes are imitating the Lord Jesus Christ, so Leighton Ford, Billy Graham's son-in-law, maintains: 'Jesus let his chosen people go through a process of trial-and-error many times. At the end, he gave them one more chance, and they failed . . . They went to sleep, and later denied they knew him. His strategy was not to cast them off, but to confront them, reinstate them, and entrust them with an even bigger task.'[163]

Frequently, the potential leader is the one who faces the biggest tests and crises of spirituality. Witness King David as being a prime example of God's patience with imperfect people! For instance, one who sees power-wielding as the key to maximizing one's influence for good, evidence of a fledgling leader, will often early on in ministry service struggle to submit to authority. As Bobby Clinton puts it, 'a developing leader will usually

---

[162] Harold Longenecker, *Growing Leaders by Design*, 98.
[163] Leighton Ford, *Transforming Leadership* (Downer's Grove, IL: InterVarsity Press, 1991), 280.

struggle with someone who is in authority over him. Learning submission is critical to learning what authority is, so emerging leaders must first learn to submit.'[164] Other tests may come in the areas of vision, faith, integrity, and love.

Speaking of the need to have a long leash on impatience in our dealings with the inconsistent people who work for us, allowing for failure in others, David McKenna observes: 'One of the tests of Incarnational leadership is whether or not we can appreciate and develop persons with whom we differ in personality, style, and outlook.'[165] It has been my experience that the Lord invariably sends our way as leaders those whose temperaments clash with ours – so that we might learn humility and be forced to make a conscious choice to let love cover a multitude of sins.

A word should be said about the concept of incarnational leadership mentioned in the previous quote. The idea of incarnation includes the notion that someone has left a familiar context to enter a new context: as in Christ identifying cross-culturally, if you will, with us on planet earth by leaving the realm of heaven. Such a transition usually implies humiliation (Phil. 2:6–8) – as in a missionary having to learn a new culture and a new language, in effect, starting all over again, like a baby, in terms of being vulnerable and dependent. Chandapilla sees this incarnational principle operative in the life of Christ in his way of training his disciples, too; the leader must build a bridge to his trainees, as Christ did.[166]

Making an effort to identify with the rank and file is what I observed early on to be the practice of George Verwer in the way he ran OM. Attending my first

---

[164] Bobby Clinton, *The Making of a Leader*, 13.
[165] David McKenna, *Power To Follow, Grace To Lead* (Dallas, TX: Word, 1989), 125.
[166] P.T. Chandapilla, *The Master Trainer*, 4.

international OM conference in 1971 before beginning a summer of outreach in France with them, I was inspired by the fact that a diminutive man was greeting the North Americans arriving in Brussels at the airport on a charter flight early one morning. It was George Verwer. His down-to-earth greeting of each of us did not seem to square with the significance of his role in the organization but it was inspiring and instructive of what incarnational leadership is all about.

What does incarnational leadership, defined in these terms, have to do with tolerating mistakes in followers? Just this. Incarnational leaders seek to demolish the image that they are holier-than-thou in relation to the common person. One way they demonstrate this humility is to signal through allowing their people the freedom to make mistakes that they themselves are not perfect. Wanting to receive mercy, they are merciful (Matt. 5:7).

It is calming on a team to have a leader whom you know will not boot anyone off the team for an error in judgment or a dispositional flaw. Greenleaf in his book on servant leadership describes a mid-level manager at AT&T who impressed him to no end because he tolerated his workers falling flat on their faces, seeing such incidents as being crucial to character formation.[167] The story is told of Tom Watson, founder of IBM, known for his unorthodox ways, meeting once with a junior executive who had mismanaged a risky venture, losing $10 million in the process. Expecting to be fired when he was called into Watson's office, the man nervously stuttered, 'I guess you want my resignation.' To which Watson retorted, 'You can't be serious. We've just spent $10 million educating you.'[168]

[167] Robert Greenleaf, *The Power of Servant Leadership*, 139–140.
[168] Warren Bennis and Burt Nanus, *Leaders: The Strategies for Taking Charge*, 76.

Two voices in particular have spoken out passionately against the way the church of Jesus Christ hangs its leaders out to dry after they have committed a terrible sin. One represents the two-thirds world and the other, the western world. I refer to African Gottfried Osei-Mensah, on the one hand, and American Gordon MacDonald, on the other.[169] We'll let Osei-Mensah speak for both of them.

> The church of Africa has to decide which is better. Do we want leaders who sin and who then, for fear of losing face or losing their job, fail to confess their sin, hiding it in their hearts? Such leaders are no longer in fellowship with the Lord and are therefore spiritually disqualified to lead the flock. Is that what we want? Or do we prefer leaders who walk in the light, confessing their sins and seeking the Lord's forgiveness and restoration? . . . But when leaders do confess their sin and make a new beginning, why is it that we put them out of their jobs? Are we acting according to culture or according to Scripture?[170]

One thing is certain though. If leaders expect to receive mercy, they should exercise mercy themselves, when it is in their power to withhold or to give a fresh start to lapsed followers.

Speaking of the patience needed to work with imperfect people, Chandapilla describes Christ's empathetic leadership in this way: 'Stickability is the ability of the trainer to finish the course and to hold on to the last to all his charge of trainees in effective training under great discouragements

---

[169] These viewpoints are articulated in Gottfried Osei-Mensah, *Wanted: Servant Leaders* and Gordon MacDonald, *Rebuilding Your Broken World* (Crowborough, UK: Highland Books, 1988).
[170] Ibid., 34.

and without any assured results to count upon.'[171] His patience with Peter's gross mistakes, culminating in his denial of his Lord three times on the night of his crucifixion, is but one vivid example of granting grace-oriented latitude to those whom we lead (John 21:15–19). The leader must not give up on his or her people the way the followers might on their leader. Perhaps this longsuffering quality is what Proverbs 20:28 had in mind thousands of years ago in wisely discerning that 'love and faithfulness keep a king safe; through love his throne is made secure' (cf. Prov. 17:17). Make no mistake, waiting for people to outgrow their foibles and flaws pays enormous dividends in the long run in most cases.

Admitting weakness and being open to criticism

Related to being a leader who tolerates weaknesses in followers is having the knack of admitting personal weaknesses and being open to criticism oneself. It is one thing to be big-hearted when it concerns others and another thing to not have a shrivelled heart when you bear the brunt of the criticism or hostility. Such a capacity to be the subject of negativity demands a self-confidence even more than working with people who do not make you look good because their work is riddled with mediocrity. Leighton Ford makes exactly this point in persuading that Christ did not become a servant out of any sense of personal weakness, for he was deeply secure in his self-identity.[172] Indeed, it could be said of Christ that 'when they hurled insults at him, he did not retaliate; when he suffered, he made no threats' (1 Peter 2:23; cf. Isaiah 50:6). He was able to handle criticism.

---

[171] P.T. Chandapilla, *The Master Trainer*, 55.

[172] Leighton Ford, *Transforming Leadership*, 153.

All too frequently though we have had the *déjà vu* sense of dealing with leaders who posture strength and invincibility, but which we suspect is not true of them. Such leaders have a tendency to run away from problems rather than to deal with them because they are more committed to not looking bad than to getting godly results. Servant leadership though is disregarding about reputation (not that a bad one is preferred), being more concerned with integrity. In one sense we have already addressed this issue in comparing a short-term to a long-term mentality, in the last subsection. The conflict between Absalom and King David serves as an example of when a willingness to admit error in judgment would have led to a restored relationship and the end to a tragedy of epic proportions. Leaders should have the humility to admit their mistakes (Matt. 18:15). Poking fun at the self-importance of bosses, Kanter spells out typical knee-jerk reactions of leaders to problems as follows.

- Regard any new idea from below with suspicion.
- Ask departments or individuals to challenge each other's proposals.
- Insist that people who need your approval to act first go through several other areas of management to get their signature.
- Express your criticisms freely and withhold your praise.
- Control everything carefully.
- Spring changes on people unexpectedly to keep them on their toes.
- Don't give out information too freely.
- Don't forget that as the boss you automatically know everything important about the business.[173]

---

[173] Rosabeth Moss Kanter, *The Change Masters*, 101.

Sometimes exhibiting the vulnerability that is suggestive of not hiding personal weakness is non-verbal. Shedding tears publicly among men is considered, at least in most western cultures, as a sign of weakness. Yet it is striking to discover how many great men of God down through church history were known for allowing their tears to flow in a public setting. In the present day, George Verwer is one. Charles Spurgeon of a century ago was known for weeping in the pulpit. However, we have no higher authority than the Lord Jesus Christ himself who wept at the graveside of Lazarus and over the spiritual state of Jerusalem, and not in private, for these incidents are recorded for us in Scripture. Call this transparency. It is the quality of a master trainer, one whose unreserved self-exposure will motivate followers to learn from the example presented.[174] Chandapilla says it well: 'A person who wants to shut up his inner life from others, who enjoys being alone and having personal privacy or who wants to be a recluse should not enter into the programme of leadership training. Such a person may have fans or admirers but he cannot reproduce himself in others. Reproducing oneself and building up others are basic to the Christian programme because Christianity is a communal faith and not merely a personal religion of the individual.'[175]

A leader who wants to do his or her best will not rebuff criticism when it comes.[176] A willingness to learn from criticism will actually invite more criticism because people will realize that they will not be penalized when they correct their leader. Not always is negative feedback indicative of fault in the leader. Sometimes it just represents a different point of view. A teachable leader discerns this difference

[174] P.T. Chandapilla, *The Master Trainer*, 27–31.
[175] Ibid., 32.
[176] John Stott, 'What Makes Leadership Christian?', 26.

and so learns to sift through negative input so as to benefit from a perspective that is constructively different from one's own. A teachable spirit is commended in Scripture, as in Proverbs 9:7–9, where it is viewed as being indicative of wisdom. Covey calls this 'empathetic listening [which] gets inside the other's frame of reference'.[177] When we accept that our security comes from the Lord and not ourselves, we develop the grace to weather the storm of negativity so that we can sift through it for the nuggets of gold which help us to improve in our job or character. Without allowing ourselves to become lightning rods for followers' discontent, we remain impervious to blind spots in our leadership. As George Mallone rightly observes: 'Rejection is part of the leader's portfolio.'[178]

Fear of rejection poses a dilemma for leaders. Just as King David's public revealing of deep emotions as he danced before the Lord resulted in the scorn of his wife, Michal, we run the risk of alienating our followers if we reveal too much about our innermost selves too quickly. One thinks of the words of Christ not to cast pearls before swine. Nevertheless, we must take risks in the area of transparency for the sake of training and influencing those who count on us to blaze the trail. Chandapilla recognizes Christ's gradual revealing of himself to his disciples along the pathway of transparency and has this to say about that transparency of Christ: 'Transparency is that quality of a master-trainer which enables him to open and expose himself in full measure, without any reservation to his charge in a manner that the trainees understand till they know him through and through.'[179]

---

[177] Stephen Covey, *Principle-Centered* Leadership, 240.

[178] George Mallone, *Furnace of Renewal: A Vision for the Church* (Downer's Grove, IL: InterVarsity Press, 1981), 89.

[179] P.T. Chandapilla, *The Master Trainer*, 27.

Ah, yes, transparency. Another way to describe an openness to admitting one's mistakes in front of others. Surely we would have to treat transparency as being one of the attributes of God. Theologians will refer to God's willingness to reveal himself to humankind as immanency. Its opposite is transcendency, also one of God's attributes. He is far above all and cannot be reduced to finite terms, and yet he is also Immanuel, 'God with us'. The self-disclosing nature of God is couched in language like 'in him is no darkness' (1 John 1:5). His truthfulness is one of the offshoots of this characteristic. No wonder then that he is described as hating human deceptiveness (Psalm 18:26) on the one hand and being pleased with the openness reflective of genuine repentance on the other (Psalm 66:18). The unveiling of Jesus, although gradual, enabled humankind to adequately understand who God is (John 1:14).

Transparency means being ourselves around other people. The humanity of the leader is something followers yearn to see. Miller put this principle accordingly: 'Openness is an almost imperative quality in a leader's life. Those who live in openness survive mistakes the best.'[180] That refreshing openness explains, in part, what made Martin Luther so magnetic to his theological students. Even at an advanced age, for example, Luther freely admitted that other women could turn his eye. No wonder he overthrew celibacy with his marriage. He had a mug with three rings on it. The first he said represented the ten commandments, the second the Apostles' Creed, and the third the Lord's Prayer. He then proceeded to boast that he could drain his mug of beer through the Lord's Prayer though his friends could not get beyond the ten commandments. Never drunk, he was nevertheless

---

[180] Calvin Miller, *Leadership*, 94.

sometimes depressed and ill. He never hid who he was around his students.

Or one thinks of Charles Spurgeon who was considered the greatest English language preacher of the nineteenth century, speaking regularly to crowds of twenty thousand in the Metropolitan Tabernacle in London. Nonetheless, he was not one to hide from his people the periods of despair that he sometimes fell into. Of this despair he said, 'There are dungeons beneath the Castle of Despair'.[181] Although possessing an impressive library of twelve thousand books, Spurgeon, with self-deprecating humour, observed that 'affliction ... is the best book in a minister's library'[182], perhaps being reminded of how he and his wife were constantly unwell, he being bothered by gout, and in 1879, needing a five month physical break. Servant leaders do not take themselves too seriously: poking fun at oneself is a form that transparency takes. Great leaders seem to have this ability to be irreverent or non-secretive about themselves.

Speaking about this willingness of the leader to openly express feelings, in other words, to be transparent, Thomas Quick has this to say in describing how crucial this is in team communications in the corporate world: 'A strong insistence on rationality [in a work team] also indicates an uneasiness with openness, even fear. People who deny emotions, in themselves or in others, feel vulnerable. They don't wish to communicate as whole people. In fact, much communication is non-rational – that is, intuitive and emotional.'[183]

---

[181] Arnold A. Dallimore, *Spurgeon* (Edinburgh: The Banner of Truth Trust, 1995), 186.
[182] Victor Shepherd, *So Great A Cloud of Witnesses* (Toronto: Light and Life Press Canada, 1993), 63.
[183] Thomas L. Quick, *Successful Team Building* (New York: American Management Association, 1992), 63.

The last word on this aspect of vulnerability goes again to writer and pastor, Calvin Miller: 'There is one final quality to develop if you genuinely wish to set yourself up to be forgiven for your mistakes. You must communicate to people that you are a real human being, and, like all the world around you, are a person in process. Process people are much easier to forgive when they are caught in error than those who try to project that they are complete and full of wisdom. The right to grow is an important right.'[184]

Trusting others in your absence

It took me almost a decade of missions' executive leadership for me to notice that when I returned from a long trip I was internally very angry my first day or two back in the office. Part of that was no doubt due to the mountain of paper and people work which had piled up in my absence (e-mail had not yet been invented!). But any little initiative taken in my absence by the office manager or a department head seemed to rub me the wrong way. As I got in touch with the feelings produced by a two or three week absence from my headquarters' team, I realized that my paranoia was caused by a personal insecurity about my leadership. I doubt whether others noticed my touchiness, or if they did, understood what the cause was. Seeing this pattern in my behaviour led me to do a lot of soul-searching. In retrospect, I can see that something was lacking in my motivation to lead from a servant's perspective. Perhaps I clung to power too much for its own sake and so was protective of anything that might be construed as a threat to my power's preservation.

---

[184] Calvin Miller, *Leadership*, 95.

Vulnerability, then, in this case, means holding to the reins of power lightly. I mean, really. What is the likelihood of a coup occurring on evangelical turf? And if it happens, so what! Better to find out what sort of people you are working with or how poor your leadership is early on rather than later, after all the damage has been done! The way a leader handles his or her absences, then, is telling about their level of servant leadership.

What a contrast to insecure leadership the apostle Paul demonstrated. He seemed to have been quite comfortable with prolonged absences from the ministries he had birthed or to what he had given in-depth leadership. He dealt with problems in churches he founded or sought to exercise apostolic authority not by decree but by establishing broad theological principles which then had to be applied with maturity by local elders (e.g. as found in Romans 13 and 14).[185]

Of course, one of the ways we demonstrate trust in co-workers and a commitment to holding to power lightly is to be good delegators. We have already given some thought to that subject. As Lao-tzu observed: 'The wise leader does not intervene unnecessarily. The leader's presence is felt, but often the group runs itself.'[186]

Planning for your succession

It is well understood that many organizations and ministries thrive in their first generation of leadership because of the dynamism of their founder, but languish thereafter because (1) the founder has shoes to fill that

---

[185] Don Howell, 'Confidence in the Spirit as the Governing Ethos of the Pauline Mission', 37ff.
[186] Lao-tzu, 'Tao Te Ching', 70.

are not easily filled, or (2) the founder fails to select and train his or her successor, often holding onto the reins of power beyond the point of usefulness. Thus it is not surprising to find Finzel identifying this failure to crown success with succession as being one of the top ten mistakes that leaders make.[187] He sees the ideas listed below as being the barriers that prevent too many leaders from grooming their successors from early on in their tenure.

- *Job security:* What am I going to do next?
- *Fear of retirement:* Me, retire?
- *Resistance to change:* The saddle is so comfortable.
- *Self-worth:* This role is my whole life.
- *Lack of confidence:* Who else can do this job like I do?
- *Love for the job:* I really love my leadership role.
- *Loss of investment:* I've put too much into this group to let it go.[188]

What strikes you in looking at this list of fears? How little these attitudes demonstrate a servant's heart, surely. Generosity of spirit means putting the group's interests above my own. To plan for your succession the day you begin requires a vulnerability that many leaders are afraid to risk. Announcing your intentions can make you a lame duck leader. It can lead to office politics as cabals are formed. Yet servant leaders will take such risks. The former president of Coca-Cola was one of them. Roberto Goizueta was the CEO of Coca-Cola for 16 years. One of his greatest achievements was his mentoring of a cadre of potential successors. When he lay on his deathbed suffering from terminal lung cancer, he made an unusual statement. He said, 'If you want to worry about me, that

---

[187] Hans Finzel, *The Top Ten Mistakes Leaders Make*, 158–177.
[188] Ibid., 164.

is okay, but don't worry about the company. When I die, the company will be in better hands than ever.'[189] He had put the company's well-being above his own, planning well for his departure.

As we have already seen, Moses was one such far-sighted leader. He prepared Joshua to take over from him as the Israelites' leader years before it happened, as the book of Deuteronomy reveals. In spite of his greatness, Moses was not too self-important to remember his own mortality. He had heeded the advice that Finzel well articulates: 'We must not get too wrapped up in our own indispensability. Humility is the key to finishing well.'[190]

My observation over many years of travelling or living extensively in the two-thirds world is that there especially we find that Christian leaders hold onto power too long and that this tendency is found in epidemic proportions.[191] Reflecting on the contrarian example of the apostle Paul, Ghanian Osei-Mensah notes: 'Would to God that we would learn this [unselfish example of Paul] in Africa today. Our national leaders want to stay in office until they drop dead, and when they drop dead nobody has been prepared to take over for them. It is the same in the church.'[192]

In my previous book I made an extended reference to a national church planting movement started by Bakht Singh, a Sikh convert, who died in 2000 at the age of 97.

---

[189] Quoted in R. Leslie Holmes, 'Be Sure To Leave Your Light On!', *Ministry* (November 1998), 6.
[190] Hans Finzel, *The Top Ten Mistakes Leaders Make*, 171.
[191] I admit that I am generalizing in this statement, and that there are factors that exacerbate such tendencies in the two-thirds world, like rampant unemployment, whereas westerners can more easily flit from one job to another.
[192] Gottfried Osei-Mensah, *Wanted: Servant Leaders*, 55.

What I failed to mention was that although this is a celebrated instance of an indigenous Christian movement, there has been a fly in the ointment. For the better part of his final decade, Bakht Singh had been increasingly senile and so unable to provide the executive leadership for the several hundred churches which looked to him for guidance. That wouldn't be so bad except that he failed to name or train a successor prior to his mental decline. As a result, there has been an undercurrent of confusion and instability at the head assembly in Hyderabad, where their vaunted leader lived. There is an Indian proverb germane to this situation. It says that nothing grows under a banyan tree.

Accepting the burden of higher expectations

Ironically, even while church members do not pay their pastors on a level commensurate with their own salaries or wages, they place higher expectations on them than they do on themselves. The pastor is expected to work longer hours, be more spiritual, and make constant sacrifices, be they related to privacy or family. The same holds true for the Christian executive. The long and the short of it is that many capable and called people walk away from the ministry because they cannot cope with the high expectations placed upon them by the people they serve. Bitterness, anger and health problems are some of the perennial by-products of this pressure. Yet this pressure of being subject to double standards goes with the territory. The servant is not greater than his master. If Jesus had to suffer ignobly and had nowhere to lay his head, then can we expect fair treatment all the time? To be philosophical about the pressure of the undue expectations placed on leaders is to be invested with a generosity of spirit that endures the vulnerability such a mantle places on one.

It means living with the pressure that you can be removed justifiably from your job more easily than a lesser light could be for the same failure. It means being harder on yourself in terms of strict moral standards than you are on others. Is this wise counsel I am offering you? As much as it is true that we are all sinners saved by grace and that all gifts are necessary for the upbuilding of the body, it is also true that Scripture seems to impose a special standard on leaders. Such is the implication, for instance, of James 3:1, which advises reluctance to enter a teaching (public profile position) ministry because those who are teachers will be more strictly judged. In other words, there are graduations in expectations of moral rectitude with respect to ministry. In the same vein, in the list of qualifications for elders and deacons in 1 Timothy 3, it states that 'the overseer must be above reproach' (v. 2). Moreover, 'he must have a good reputation with outsiders' (v. 7). Similarly, deacons 'are to be men worthy of respect' (v. 8), as are their wives (or deaconesses, v. 11). Striking a solemn note along the same lines is the blunt statement of Hebrews 13:17: 'Obey your leaders and submit to their authority. They keep watch over you as men who must give an account.' In this spirit, then, Oswald Sanders, one-time International Director of Overseas Missionary Fellowship and president of a Bible College in New Zealand, made this statement: 'No one need aspire to leadership in the work of God who is not prepared to pay a price greater than his contemporaries and colleagues are willing to pay. True leadership always exacts a heavy toll on the whole man, and the more effective the leadership is, the higher the price to be paid.'[193]

---

[193] Oswald Sanders, *Spiritual Leadership*, 104.

In his most autobiographical NT letter, 2 Corinthians, Paul reveals the cost of Christian leadership to himself: 'We are hard pressed on every side, but not crushed; perplexed but not in despair; persecuted, but not abandoned; struck down, but not destroyed' (4:8–9). Paul knew the cross which comes with leadership but he also did not walk away from his ministry because of the resilience which comes from God's grace and having a servant's heart. In fact, later on in the same letter he itemizes a fuller description of a leader's pressures and specifically associates his capacity to weather these trials with having a servant's heart. Thus he says: '. . . as servants of God we commend ourselves in every way: in great endurance; in troubles, hardships, and distresses . . .' (6:4). A sign of servant leadership, then, is allowing yourself to be made vulnerable due to the expectations others place upon you.

Loneliness at the top

Related to facing higher expectations from others, leaders find themselves isolated from their colleagues oftentimes. Lonely indeed it can be at the top. There are several types of loneliness peculiar to the leader. One is physical. That is to say, generally speaking, at least in parachurch ministry, considerable travel is part of the job description. For 21 of my thirty years in the ministry, I have had to be on the road (as measured by being away from home overnight) 20–25 per cent of the year. This can take its toll on marriage and family life, although I have been blessed with a wife of like-mindedness and tremendous love for me so that these absences have not hurt our marriage. Whether visiting Canadian missionaries on the field, attending international leaders' meetings, or speaking in churches and schools around the world, I have faced many a sleepless or lonely night.

Then there is the loneliness of needing to be careful with whom you share your innermost feelings. Arising out of the ashes of his moral failure, American Christian leader Gordon MacDonald wrote a book, *Rebuilding Your Broken World*, in which, among other things, he urges those in Christian leadership to be sure that they have an account-ability relationship with someone. Whenever I have had an accountability relationship with another mature Christian of the same sex, I have found it to be a reassuring influence on me. Nevertheless, it is sometimes difficult to find such a mentor, someone mature and interested in you enough to ask you the hard questions whenever you meet and to simultaneously be able to show you uncon-ditional acceptance. The fact of the matter is that, no matter what sort of support system you have in place, there are many things that you cannot share with others by virtue of being a leader, such as the burdens and details of deep-set problems shared with you in a counselling context.

Thirdly, there is the loneliness that comes with having to make certain decisions in isolation. Having served as a missionary, parachurch leader, and a pastor, it is my opinion that executive decisions made independent of consultation are more likely to have to be made in or-ganizational (parachurch) leadership roles than in the other situations in view here. Nevertheless, there is a dynamic involved in senior leadership roles, regardless of the context, that requires leaders to be one step ahead of their followers, and to sometimes be forced because of foresight or discernment to stand by an unpopular decision that has to be made. I shall never forget the one and only time I ever had to cut allowances for home staff in our missions' headquarters. We were building up a hefty deficit as a field. Our philosophy had always been to cut ministry expenses before personal benefits of our workers. However, every ingenuity of budget-cutting and self-discipline had not reversed the flow of red ink. Complicating the problem was that two-thirds of our total budget – as it is in most organizations and churches – was related to personnel costs (like salaries and benefits). Not surprisingly, the allowance cuts were met with resistance. To this day, though, I believe I made the right decision – even though it gave me an unwanted reputation in some quarters in the organization. Of the same mind is Sanders in his statement that 'the leader must be a man who, while welcoming the friendship and support of all who can offer it, has sufficient inner resources to stand alone, even in the face of fierce opposition, in the discharge of his responsibilities'.[194]

Not only in Christian leadership (although this is the realm of leadership we are mostly concerned about in this book), but in the secular workplace, leaders can be lonely figures. Such was the case, for example, with Franco Bernabe in his six-year tenure as CEO of ENI, Italy's mammoth energy production company. During his term in office, Bernabe transformed the company from a debt-ridden, government-owned organization into a competitive and publicly-traded company.[195] To do this, however, he had to engage in some drastic and unpopular measures, like selling two hundred companies, and dismissing hundreds of managers. We might assume that a trouble-shooter like Bernabe relished his heavy-handed style of leadership. Yet he confided to hating

---

[194] Ibid., 108.
[195] Linda Hill and Suzy Wetlauffer, 'Leadership When There Is No One To Ask: An Interview With ENI's Franco Bernabe', *Harvard Business Review* (July/August 1998), 81–94.

conflict and having to be in the limelight.[196] Summing up
how he made the impossible happen, his interviewers said,

> Perhaps more than anything else, Bernabe's power to lead
> comes from within. It flows, he says, from an inner compass
> pointed toward humanity and justice. In difficult times,
> Bernabe seeks consultation from others. But ultimately, he
> makes all important decisions alone so as not to be buffeted
> by the needs, emotions, or agendas of others. Such solitude,
> he believes, is one of the burdens – and necessities – of
> leadership.[197]

Having the buck stop with me brings with it a built-in
loneliness. Servant leaders are willing to pay the price of
loneliness – as indeed they are of every other negative
component of leadership mentioned in this chapter.
Generosity of spirit is a common theme associated with
this kind of leader, the grace that permits one to be
vulnerable, to be weak instead of always strong. Such is
the stuff of which servant leadership is made.

Conclusion

If we do live on a planet of ever-increasing complexity and
speed of change, as most futurists insist, then the leader of
the future needs to be teachable. He or she needs to be able
to handle the ambiguity that comes with uncertainty and
detect what the Holy Spirit is up to in the face of chaos,
just like the men of Issachar of old of whom their epitaph
read: '[They were] men who understood the times and
knew what Israel should do . . .' (1 Chron. 12:32).

---

[196] Ibid., 83–84.
[197] Ibid., 84.

6

Vitality: Leading from the Source that is higher than I

How intriguing it is to discover that three of the towering figures of the twentieth century church shared the same experience: they were imprisoned and met with God in a special way as a result of the solitude and suffering their prison life imposed on them. Chuck Colson, Alexander Solzhenitsyn, and Dietrich Bonhoeffer, out of their extremity cried out, like the Psalmist, 'Lead me to the rock that is higher than I' (Psalm 61:2), and so discovered an enlargement of the soul that enabled them to rise to greatness. In like manner, any leader who aspires to servant leadership soon learns that contrary forces undermine the resilience of the soul needed to sustain that self-sacrificing mindset and so develops spiritual watchfulness forged out of a deepening relationship with the Lord. Although this is not a book on spiritual formation – as much as that would be an invaluable focus in discussing leadership – it would be remiss of me to omit some discussion of the significance of this aspect of the leader's behaviour. Just as affability and generosity of spirit are seen in all genuine servant leaders, you will find the trait of maintaining personal vitality, be that in the spiritual, physical, emotional, or mental realms, as a life habit in them, no matter what their style of leadership or type of leadership. Just as a lake will spread out no higher than the streams feeding into it, so the overseer can lead no more spiritually than he or she is filled with the Holy Spirit.

Whether talking about the business world or pastoring, effective leaders seem to exhibit this common trait of drawing deeply from the wells of renewing activities or disciplines. Stephen Covey identifies vitality-seeking as one of the seven indispensable habits of the effective person and calls it 'sharpening the saw'.[198] Just as priming the pump allows water to flow freely and easily, so taking the time for personal renewal through daily qualitative times alone with God, through doing such things as contrasting desk work with running thrice weekly, or carving out space and time to read a book a week allows one to minister from the overflow of an enriched life.[199]

This recharging of the batteries, to change the metaphor, means that, for example, under the pressures of leadership, you can resist the temptation to revert to the shortcut of leading in an authoritarian way. 1 Peter 5:2,3 teaches that servant and authoritarian leadership are diametrically opposed because they are contrasted with each other in this passage. 'Be shepherds of God's flock that is under your care, *serving* as overseers – not because you must, but because you are willing, as God wants you to be; not greedy for money, but *eager to serve*; not lording it over those entrusted to you, but being examples to the flock' (italic letters my addition). Note,

---

[198] Stephen Covey, *The 7 Habits of Highly Effective People* (New York: Simon & Schuster, 1990).

[199] I use these two examples of renewing activities because they are ones I practise and so can testify to as to their ability to renew – over time.

first of all, that Peter uses the word 'elders' (v. 1), 'shepherds' (v. 2), and 'overseers' (v. 2) interchangeably, thereby underscoring the multiplicity of roles in leadership in the church. The fact that these terms used to describe leaders are in the plural form is also noteworthy; a plurality of leadership in the local church is envisaged. Notice too, as we elaborated in an earlier chapter, the power of the example of the servant leader. The phrase 'not lording it over those entrusted to your care', finally, is directly contrasted with eager-to-serve leadership. You can be a strong leader, that is, authoritative, but that must be tempered with gentleness and sensitivity toward the people you oversee so that you are not authoritarian, that is, not heavy-handed in the way you relate to people out of sheer tunnel vision to get the job done at any cost. What I am trying to say here is that it is amazing how taking care of yourself provides the vitality to remain a servant leader under pressure. Greenleaf has much the same thing in mind when he says, 'One's confidence in a leader rests, in part, on the assurance that stability and poise and resilience under stress give adequate strength for the rigors of leadership.'[200] Interestingly enough, this management consultant, long connected with AT&T, at the age of seventy five, finally came to the understanding that he could serve others best 'by being'.[201] In a similar vein, William Pollard, a Christian and former CEO of the Fortune five hundred company ServiceMaster, argues, 'leaders must set the pace as both teachers and learners'.[202]

Expanding on this insight, he says the following: 'Executives who seek comfort in the experience of past successes and do not flood their lives with reading,

---

[200] Robert Greenleaf, *The Power of Servant Leadership*, 131.
[201] Ibid., 269.
[202] William Pollard, *The Soul of the Firm*, 114.

listening, teaching, testing, and new experiences are soon arrogant in their ignorances and are not leading the firm as a learning environment . . . The firm, then, is like a university, and continuous learning is an integral part of its vitality.'[203] Or consider the observation of management writer Burt Nanus: 'Visionary leaders are virtual learning machines, skilled at accumulating ideas and knowledge from a great variety of sources and putting them together in novel ways to discern patterns and directions.'[204]

One of the things that leaders who take pains to keep fresh have learned, perhaps by observing colleagues or those with whom they have grown up and are still in touch with, is that there is a levelling off tendency. Whom do you know who is at least forty years old who still pursues the acquisition of knowledge or understanding with the same zest as they did when they were twenty? Sadly, such people are the exception more than the rule. Middle-aged people too frequently rest on what they already know. Even while our society reinvents itself every five years or so, the majority of baby boomers and builders have become virtually brain dead. Instead of burning with a passion to become like Jesus a little bit more each day (speaking of the Christian variety here), adding a line here, a precept there (Is. 28:10–13), their testimony is ancient history!

Let us look, then, at specific ways of seeking after vitality. We shall see that, although not offering herein an exhaustive list of renewing disciplines, servant leaders will acquire the life habits of waiting on God daily, reading widely and deeply, carving out time for solitude regularly, keeping physically active, and practising a Sabbath rest.

---

[203] Ibid.
[204] Burt Nanus, *Visionary Leadership*, 182.

Waiting on God daily

Although it might be considered a truism to refer to the quiet time, personal devotions – call it what you will – as an indispensable aspect of discipleship, let alone leadership, you would be surprised at how many Christian leaders have an impoverished or almost non-existent devotional life. They, through the pressure of the work and competing priorities, allow their relationship with the Lord to get squeezed out, so that they become calendar Christians, getting their daily spiritual fix from a Scripture verse on a wall calendar, or a devotional reading out of Oswald Chambers or Daily Bread.

Ah yes, the bane of busyness. How often would I have to admit that the good has kept me from the best. It took a burnout of mega-proportions to get my attention as to the foolhardiness of burning the candle at both ends. While my devotional life was not particularly suspect, I was neglecting my family and self-development in other than overtly spiritual areas. More about that shortly. But first let us see what other Christian leaders have to say about how we miss out on long-term excellence in service to the Lord because we take short-cuts which sap our vitality. John Stott makes such an observation in these words:

> Enter discipline – the final mark of a Christian leader. Not only self-discipline in general (in the mastery of passions, time, and energies), but in particular the discipline with which one waits on God. The leader knows his weakness. He knows the greatness of his task and the strength of the opposition. But he also knows the inexhaustible riches of God's grace . . . Only those who discipline themselves to seek God's face will keep their vision bright.[205]

---

[205] John Stott, 'What Makes Leadership *Christian*?', 27.

Another pastor, this one on the other side of the Atlantic, makes a similar statement: 'But the word *busy* is the symptom not of commitment but of betrayal. It is not devotion but defection. The adjective *busy* set as a modifier to *pastor* should sound to our ears like *adulterous* to characterize a wife or *embezzling* to describe a banker. It is an outrageous scandal, a blasphemous affront.'[206]

In January 1980 I went through a partial nervous breakdown. There were a number of precipitating causes, but almost certainly the predominant one was the pressure I placed on myself knowing I was the first Executive Director for Canada of Arab World Ministries at the relatively tender age of thirty.[207] Inheriting a minuscule financial and missionary base, I felt as if I was keeping one step ahead of the poor house or dissolution. That first year I spoke in 150 meetings across Canada to get the name of the mission on the map of churches, Christian student campus groups, and Bible colleges. It seemed like I forgot how to relax, often skipping a day off to catch up on this or that. Without exploring the feelings and thoughts that eventually led to my deep-set depression, let me say that I had to take a short leave of absence from my ministry. I reached the point where I did not feel like getting out of bed in the morning, I dreaded meeting people, I was terrified of speaking publicly lest I be found out, and I felt awful guilt about letting my wife and young son down.

Probably I would have recovered more quickly if I had received different advice, and looked for another line of work, at least temporarily, but providentially, the self-help therapy I practised gave me unforgettable insight into God's sovereignty and the role that balanced living

---

[206] Eugene Peterson, *The Contemplative Pastor*, 17.

[207] The mission was known at that time as North Africa Mission.

plays in protecting our emotional and spiritual health. Basically the philosophy it taught me was that you get better according to how much mental pain you are willing to bear while functioning normally. Much mental illness is a function of imposing unrealistic expectations on oneself, I was told. Gradually the fears and internal torment would subside as I practised this method, in effect, ignoring my feelings while 'moving my muscles' in normal activity. Again, I must stress, though, that recovery of this nature holds true only if you avoid exceptionality behaviour, that is, learn to function normally.[208] My exceptionality lay in treating myself, in effect, as the saviour of the world. AWM depended on my hard work and far-reaching vision to survive, I had deluded myself into thinking. Now I was only being allowed to work a forty-hour week, forced to develop a hobby, spend more time with the family, and start a physical exercise regimen. These were foreign ideas for one whose missions' environment emphasized denying self and taking up one's cross daily.

Developing new habits was painful at first. I felt extremely guilty initially at working so few hours when I was 'doing God's work'. I started jogging – which has continued to this day, a 10–15 kilometer running regimen three times a week. I took up collecting stamps, and when our family moved to a detached house, I exchanged that for gardening. Some years later I added golf to the list of relaxing and physically renewing activities I engaged in regularly, something I still try to do once a week when

---

[208] I am also assuming that there is not a chemical basis for the disorder, something that can easily be tested for and which, if diagnosed, needs to be treated in a different way. Not that there cannot be a clear-cut moral issue that needs repentance from in order for inner healing to occur.

the weather co-operates. I also expanded my reading to include non-theological or non-devotional literature, becoming an avid courtroom drama suspense fan.

What does this have to do with waiting on God? My comments above seem on the contrary to be undermining the establishing of that principle. Just this. Perhaps the greatest enemy of waiting on God is workaholism. For some people to bring their life back into balance so that they don't end up reaping what they have sown in the way of self-abuse, they may need to make new efforts to spend quality time with the Lord in the word and prayer every day. To others it may be to stop and smell the roses more frequently, whether by honouring the day of rest principle regularly or to actually take those holidays owed. To still others it may be to overcome the sedentary nature of their work by beginning a physical fitness routine so as to avoid dying of heart disease at the age of sixty. As it relates to the immediate topic, the temptation to be seduced by the importance of one's role as a Christian leader by being preoccupied with the demands of the work, can only be a recipe for a long-term spiritual desert storm. We self-important leaders need to remind ourselves that Mary got the Lord's commendation over Martha and that unless the Lord builds the house, they labour in vain who build it. You know, the funny thing is, during my several years of 'downsitting', when I was working at half speed for AWM, the ministry continued to grow and prosper. God's grace is made perfect in our weakness, you see.

Even as I write this chapter, I have noticed out of the corner of my eye, so to speak, an article in my local newspaper which describes the head of one of Canada's largest companies, Alcan, quitting his job overnight because he was on the verge of burnout. Known for his gruelling pace of working 12-hour days seven days a week and being constantly jet-lagged from travelling to Alcan locations around the world, this executive constantly talked about how he as the CEO had to set the pace if he expected others and the company itself to perform according to shareholder expectations. He embodied just what we are trying to avoid in this chapter, by preaching moderation in all things.

In setting aside a deliberate time each day to let God speak to us through his word and we to him in prayer, especially in the morning waking hours, we are renewing the practice of men and women of Bible times. Thus in Psalm 5:3 we are told that David waited on the Lord in the morning (cf. Ps. 57:8; 119:147–8). Other Old Testament saints practised this spiritual discipline too (Gen. 19:27; 22:3; Ps. 88:13; Ex. 24:4). However, the New Testament example *par excellence* was Christ himself who often got up to be alone with his heavenly Father before the crack of dawn (e.g. Mark 1:35).

It may not be, as I have discovered, that one meets with God in a profound way very often in the quiet time, but just knowing that the habit of listening does produce results occasionally keeps you coming back for more. Not uncommonly people I know who have fallen out of the habit of maintaining this daily ritual cite the dryness of the routine as a main factor in their dropping it, or irregularly keeping it. But one must keep at it to benefit from it. The alternative is worse: to discover one day that God is no longer there or that you do not have the inner resources to marshall in coping with a difficult situation or temptation. Thus it is that Dietrich Bonhoeffer could make this bold statement: 'The prayer of the morning will determine the day. Wasted time, which we are ashamed of, temptations that beset us, weakness and listlessness in our work, disorder and indiscipline in our thinking and our relations with other people very frequently have their cause in the neglect of our morning prayer.'[209]

Speaking more narrowly of the importance of this spiritual discipline for the pastor (after all, we are specifically addressing Christian leaders in this book), Bonhoeffer goes on to say,

> Since meditation on the Scriptures, prayer, and intercession are a service we owe and because the grace of God is found in this service, we should train ourselves to set apart a regular hour for it, as we do for every other service we perform. This is not 'legalism', it is orderliness and fidelity. For most people the early morning will prove to be the best time. We have a right to this time, even prior to the claims of our people, and we may insist on having it as a completely undisturbed quiet time despite all external difficulties. For the pastor it is an indispensable duty, and his whole ministry will depend on it. Who can really be faithful in great things if he has not learned to be faithful in the things of daily life?[210]

Lately I have been using a Bible I had laid aside for some years. Until recent years I have been in the habit of putting the date and a short note in the column of the Bible beside a verse that I sense the Lord has particularly spoken to me through. In reading through this old Bible, I have marvelled afresh at the breadth and depth of the topics and situations I have been touched by in a timely way – all as I have gone about the simple business of having a quiet time. It has occurred to me that the mature comprehension of my own frailty and fallenness has been shaped, to a large extent, by these daily readings in

---

[209] Dietrich Bonhoeffer, *Life Together*, 71.

[210] Ibid., 87.

God's word. Hence I find myself agreeing with Tom Marshall's assessment that 'servant leaders have genuine humility of heart and because of that a realistic and sound judgement as to their capabilities and their deficiencies, the things they can do well and the things they can do not'.[211]

It is not my intent here to expound on the way to go about the spiritual discipline of spending time alone with God daily. But two aspects of it are relevant to the purpose of this chapter. They are to (1) be creative in finding ways to keep your quiet time fresh, and (2) never forget that the spiritual life requires embodiment and therefore specific, God-ordained disciplines, in order to flourish.

Here are several variations I have introduced to my quiet time over the years in order to keep it vital. While in India as a young adult, I was influenced by participation in a George Verwer Intensive Training Programme (similar to an Outward Bound programme but with a spiritual twist) to read through the Bible once every year. There were many other requirements of the programme but this one stuck. On and off, since then, I do that as part of my quiet time. It mitigates against being reflective and meditative in Bible reading, but since I am currently a pastor I find that I have ample opportunity to engage in the more in-depth aspect of Bible study. However, extensive reading does introduce you to the grand sweep of biblical themes and the character of God in a way that intensive reading can fail to do. Otherwise, I try to read a Psalm or a Proverb every day so that I complete those two devotional and practical books twice every year. Always too, a chapter in the NT. I also vary translations, and now have read the Bible or NT in about twelve different versions.

---

[211] Tom Marshall, *Understanding Leadership: Fresh Perspectives on the Essentials of New Testament Leadership* (Chichester, England: Sovereign World, 1991), 73.

A few years ago I began to sing a hymn or chorus in my quiet time, sensing I needed to improve in the worship side of my relationship with the Lord. Recently I completed the several hundred songs in the classic Ira Sankey hymnal in this way. Usually, as well, I read a page or so out of a devotional book – but not before I have done all my other Bible reading. Occasionally I also write thoughts in a notebook I keep alongside my Bible about how I feel God is speaking to me.

A word on meditation. There are definitely meditative elements to the quiet time. However, it should properly be treated as a separate discipline of the spirit. We are only going to relate to it here, however, as it intrudes on the quiet time. Since the Psalms in particular associate meditation with deep reflection on the word of God (e.g. Ps. 119:15), it will occur in the course of certain types of reading of Scripture. A dictionary synonym for *meditation* is *rumination*. This is what Downing has in mind in his book by that name in discussing the nature of meditation: 'Just as a ruminant animal extracts nourishment from grass or hay through chewing and transferring it into its bloodstream, so also as we meditate on the word of God we extract the life of Christ and transfer it to our spiritual bloodstream. This is the fulfillment of Jesus' statement, "It is the man who shares my life and whose life I share who proves fruitful" (John 15:5, PHILLIPS).'[212]

There are occasions when I am waiting on God early in the morning that a certain verse or phrase captures my attention to the extent that I must mull over it for some minutes before moving on. It may be a new truth breaking in on my consciousness. Or an old truth yielding new dimensions. Or the timing of being reminded of this

---

[212] Jim Downing, *Meditation* (Colorado Springs, CO: NavPress, 1976), 30.

'word' is so uncanny that I must pause there to make sure I miss nothing of the word of the Lord to my soul. It may mean tracing all the cross references showing for that verse in my Bible, reading it in other versions, breathing it out loud in prayer, or using various reflective methods I may not normally use in my daily readings in Scripture. There is always an intention to obey God in a fresh way arising out of the stillness of this piercing moment of meditation. Therefore I find myself agreeing with Thomas Merton in his assessment of what meditation is.

> To meditate is to exercise the mind in serious reflection. This is the broadest possible sense of the word 'meditation'. The term in this sense is not confined to religious reflections, but it implies serious mental activity and a certain absorption or concentration which does not permit our faculties to wander off at random or remain slack and undirected . . . Reflection involves not only the mind but also the heart, and indeed our whole being. One who really meditates does not merely think, he also loves.[213]

About half of my quiet time is spent in Bible reading and the other half in prayer and praise. Gradually over the years I have found that it helps me to concentrate in prayer if I work from a prayer list. Presently I have a different prayer list for each day of the week, some names (like my wife's and my son's) appearing on the list every day, some names every other day, and some a couple of times a week, but most only once. I also have longer lists that I use on my occasional special prayer and fasting days. From time to time, I try praying without my list but usually find that my thoughts wander too much.

---

[213] Thomas Merton, *Spiritual Direction and Meditation* (Collegeville, MN: The Liturgical Press, 1960), 52.

It has helped to remind myself of the principle I learned in OM, that prayer is hard work and so I do not have to feel like praying in order for it to have value.[214] The important thing is to be obedient (1 Tim. 2:1,2). I also use mission daily prayer sheets to intercede for organizations and ministries for which I have a special affection. These prayer sheets are bookmarks in my Bible so that as I read my OT chapter for the day, for example, in passing, I pray for the mission prayer request for that day.

Closing out this section on the quiet time, I would be remiss if I did not clarify what I mean by prayer. The longer I am a Christian the more I find myself learning the art of conversational, missile-like praying. The kind that Nehemiah engaged in when he breathed silently a prayer to heaven when in the presence of the king of Babylon (Neh. 2:4). Surely that is what Paul had in mind when he exhorted God's people to 'pray on all occasions' (Eph. 6:18), spontaneous prayer that occurs in the midst of the hustle and bustle of daily life and which expresses a heart-felt dependency on the living God. Systematic prayer and situational prayer must be balanced, for ultimately it is characteristic of a dynamic personal relationship with Christ. I quite agree with Thomas Merton then in his reflection on prayer: 'It is almost useless to try to recollect myself for the moment of prayer if I have allowed my senses and imagination to run wild all the rest of the day. Consequently the desire to practice meditation [as in a quiet

---

[214] This concept is confirmed by other students of spirituality, like Richard Foster, who in his classic spiritual formation book, *Celebration of Discipline*, says, 'We must never wait until we feel like praying before we will pray for others. Prayer is like any other work; we may not feel like working, but once we have been at it for a bit, we begin to feel like working' (Sevenoaks, UK: Hodder & Stoughton, 1984), 39.

time] implies the effort to preserve moderate recollection throughout the day. It means living in an atmosphere of faith and with occasional moments of prayer and attention to God.'[215]

And I agree with Dallas Willard, even though I would have to confess that my prayer life is in constant need of repair, and does not fully reflect the experience his quote implies: 'Praying with frequency gives us the readiness to pray again as needed from moment to moment. The more we pray, the more we think to pray, and as we see the results of prayer – the response of our Father to our requests – our confidence in God's power spills over into other areas of our lives.'[216]

Difficult it would be to find church leaders of any significance in any century who gave but lip service to the role of prayer and Bible reading in their acquiring of power and fruitfulness in ministry. Not surprising then do we discover that the longest chapter in John Calvin's *Institutes* is devoted to prayer (Book 3, Chapter 20). When asked what should be in the preacher's library, Richard Baxter, influential Puritan pastor, urged that it should include a Bible, concordance, commentary, catechism, something on the doctrine of the gospels, and as many devotional books as possible (he lists sixty of them).[217]

In delving into Indian church history for one of the courses I taught in Briercrest's MA Extension Degree Programme in Hyderabad, India, I traced the same characteristic through their key figures. Bishop Azariah, the first Indian bishop of the Anglican church and the

---

[215] Thomas Merton, *Spiritual Direction and Meditation*, 78.

[216] Dallas Willard, *The Spirit of the Disciplines: Understanding How God Changes Lives* (San Francisco: HarperCollins, 1991), 185.

[217] J.I. Packer, *A Quest for Godliness: The Puritan Vision of the Christian Life* (Wheaton, IL: Crossway Books, 1990).

founder of an early indigenous missionary society, for example, was reputed to regularly rise at 4:30 a.m. to have his quiet time. Commenting on his own spiritual life, he declared that 'the more one feels the ideal is far from one's experience, the more one is compelled to cast oneself on God'.[218] Every morning William Carey began his day by reading a chapter from the Bible in each of Latin, Greek, Hebrew, Dutch, French and English. Martin Luther knew much of the NT and large sections of the OT by heart, and for several years read through the Bible twice every 12 months.

Now a few thoughts about why, when our sanctification is a work of grace (1 Cor. 1:8,9; 1 Thes. 5:23,24; Rom. 8:29), we have a part to play in its unfolding too. A growing misconception of our age is that the work of the Holy Spirit instantaneously and spectacularly graces us with new power and vitality for service. But my simple answer to that is then why is so much of the NT couched in the form of commands and promises, so as to address our will and quicken our faith? Common sense, too, tells us that practice makes perfect.[219] While not wanting to be accused of being Aristotelian in my theology, for I firmly believe that it is the Holy Spirit alone, and therefore God's grace, that transforms us (2 Cor. 4:16), human spirituality also requires embodiment; God's Spirit uses our efforts, in part, as his means to bring about his sanctifying work (Phil. 2:12,13). Thus it is that Willard argues that 'the approach to wholeness is for humankind a process of great length and difficulty that engages all our powers to their fullest extent over a long course of

---

[218] Carol Graham, *Azariah of Dornakal*, (Madras, India: Christian Literature Service – revised edition, 1972), 7.

[219] I'm not denying here that salvation is by grace, that is, justification is by faith in Christ alone.

experience.'[220] Clarifying what he means by this, elsewhere he cogently argues the following.

> The secret of the standard, historically proven spiritual disciplines is precisely that they *do* respect and count on the bodily nature of human personality. They all deeply and essentially involve bodily conditions and activities. Thus they show us effectively *how* we can 'offer our bodies as living sacrifices, holy, and acceptable unto God' and how our 'spiritual worship' (Rom. 12:1) really is inseparable from the offering up of our bodies in specific physical ways. Paul's teachings, especially when added to his practices, strongly suggest that he understood and practiced something vital about the Christian life that we have lost – and that we must do our best to recover.[221]

Therefore, we do not shy away from insisting that vitality in leadership is a function of undertaking certain disciplines on a consistent basis, the first one profiled here being waiting on God.

On reading widely

In the second place, crucial to my spiritual formation and sustainable vitality has been reading – reading widely and reading selectively. Modest as the goal may seem, my aim is to read one book a week. Delving into church history again to find inspirational direction on this subject, one does not have far to look. Below are but several examples of outstanding Christian leaders whose reading played a major role in their influence and impact.

---

[220] Dallas Willard, *The Spirit of the Disciplines*, 70.
[221] Ibid., 19.

1. Richard Baxter (1615–1691), although over two hundred writings of his survive (in 23 volumes), was largely self-educated. J.I. Packer calls him 'the greatest of all the Puritan pastors'.[222]

2. Jonathan Edwards (1703–1758), hailed by many as the greatest theologian the American church has ever produced, was widely read, studying thirteen hours a day. He was well read too, steeping himself in the writings of philosophers like John Locke and Isaac Newton.

3. John Wesley (1703–1791), who more than any other Englishman contributed to the religious awakening in the British Isles of the eighteenth century, and was the founder of Methodism, read one hundred books a year, much of them on horseback, as he travelled over two hundred and fifty thousand miles per year in his itinerant preaching. His journals reveal that he even read medical encyclopedias on horseback – which perhaps explains his eclectic writing output, such as penning a book for the masses on medicinal cures, and a treatise on electricity, quite apart from his theological contributions.

4. Charles Spurgeon (1834–1892) is considered to have been the greatest preacher in the English language of the nineteenth century. Everything about him was larger than life, including his massive library of twelve thousand volumes and claim to read six books a week! Although lacking a formal theological education, he founded his own well-enrolled Bible College and allegedly never repeated himself in over three thousand five hundred sermons. He consulted well over three thousand commentaries in preparing his *Commenting and Commentaries*. He read *Pilgrim's Progress* one hundred times and was well-acquainted

---

[222] J.I. Packer, *A Quest for Godliness*.

with Shakespeare, biographies, science, history, art, and poetry, as well as theology.

Why read? Well, for one thing, we are to love the Lord our God with all our 'mind', as the greatest commandment reminds us (Mk. 12:30). All truth is God's truth. He is the Creator as well as the Saviour. Our mental faculties are part of not only our physiological but of our spiritual makeup – otherwise we would not have been communicated to by the living and personal God by other than his Son incarnationally living amongst us: propositionally, then, God has revealed himself to us, appealing to our minds in his self-disclosure. He has revealed himself to us, if you will, by video, and by book. Thus we are taught in Scripture that much of the battle for spiritual perception and embracing of truth is in the mind (2 Cor. 10:3–5; Phil. 4:8). We are to be transformed *by the renewing of our minds* (Rom. 12:2).

Of course, first of all, in doing so, we must major on the book of books. However, within Scripture itself, we find illustration of the importance of developing our minds in other ways. One such model is found in the person of the apostle Paul who at the end of his life could write these words from prison: 'When you come, bring the cloak I left with Carpus at Troas, and my scrolls, especially the parchments' (2 Tim. 4:13). Paul was a life-long learner and so he craved access to not only his Bible (the scrolls) but his parchments (books were written on leather leaves by hand). We are as Christian leaders to work hard at studying the word of God (2 Tim. 3:16,17) and at keeping our minds fit in general (1 Peter 1:13; 4:7; 5:8). On this subject of whether we should concentrate in our reading on more than the Bible, Charles Spurgeon is informing.

Some of our ultra-Calvinistic brethren think that a minister who reads books and studies his sermon must be a deplorable specimen of a preacher ... The man who never reads will never be read; he who never quotes will never be quoted. He who will not use the thoughts of other men's brains, proves that he has no brains of his own. Brethren, what is true of ministers is true of all our people. YOU need to read. Renounce as much as you will all light literature, but study as much as possible sound theological works.[223]

Further insight into the power of reading to acquire knowledge and to sharpen the mental faculties of leaders is furnished by management literature. The repeated exhortation found there is that wide-scale knowledge acquisition helps leaders and their companies to predict and prepare for change. The most competitive companies are 'learning organizations' and so adapt well to change.[224] Along the same lines, Moss Kanter contends: 'Entrepreneurs – and entrepreneurial organizations – always operate at the edge of their competence, focusing more of their resources and attention on what they do not yet know ... than on controlling what they already know.'[225] Growing leaders overcome the sort of intellectual arrogance that blocks a predilection to acquiring knowledge in areas they are weak in and so learn to stretch their capacities.[226] 'The person who doesn't read is no better than the person who can't read.'[227] Leaders must be generalists but most of their higher formal learning is highly specialized and so

---

[223] Quoted in James A. Stewart, *The Treasure House of Good Books* (Edinburgh: D. Mackay & Sons, 1969), 5.

[224] Peter Senge, *The Fifth Dimension: The Art and Practice of the Learning Organization.*

[225] Rosabeth Moss Kanter, *The Change Masters*, 27.

[226] Peter Drucker, 'Managing Oneself', *Harvard Business Review* (March/April 1999), 66–67.

[227] Stephen Covey, *The 7 Habits of Highly Effective People*, 295.

they must develop the discipline to learn eclectically and interdisciplinarily.[228] In their analysis of ninety CEOs, Bennis and Nanus conclude that leaders are perpetual learners: 'Some are voracious readers ... Many learn mainly from other people ... Nearly all leaders are highly proficient in learning from experience ... All of them regard themselves as "stretching", "growing", and "breaking new ground".'[229]

Open-mindedness, ability to be objective, and capacity to think innovatively are all qualities of the mind which are improved upon through reading, and which are necessary qualities in leaders. Thus it is not surprising to find Bobby Clinton, head of the Leadership Department at Fuller Theological Seminary, one of North America's most respected evangelical seminaries, maintaining: 'One of the striking characteristics seen in effective leaders is their desire to learn. They learn from all kinds of sources ... Effective leaders, at all levels, maintain a learning posture throughout life.'[230] It is worth noting that Clinton attributes his insights on leadership development in large measure to his fascination with reading biographies.

Worth the price of the book, *Spiritual Leadership*, is Oswald Sanders' chapter called 'The Leader and His Reading'. How astute he is in making this observation: 'If it is true that a man is known by the company he keeps, it is no less true that his character is reflected in the books he reads, for they are the outward expression of his inner hungers and aspirations.'[231] As the years wear on, I find myself scanning through the bibliography of an author

---

[228] John Gardener, *On Leadership*, 159.

[229] Warren Bennis and Burt Nanus, *Leaders: The Strategies for Taking Charge*, 188.

[230] Bobby Clinton, *The Making of a Leader*, 180.

[231] Oswald Sanders, *Spiritual Leadership*, 98.

before I begin reading the book because it tells me immediately how well read he is and therefore how likely I am to benefit from the book! Occasionally I will purchase a book only on the basis of the bibliography at the back of the book. Increasingly, I also find myself drawn to some of the older theological writers, and so empathize with J.I. Packer's affinity for the Puritan divines. I also find myself rereading books which are classics, like *Pilgrim's Progress*.

Reading widely does not necessarily come easily. You do not have to be a book worm or an intellectual giant to be committed to the discipline. Leaders have a curiosity of life that must be satisfied through various types of learning. They are also driven to acquire a wide range of knowledge, being constantly surprised at what ideas and insights they can put to work, and so even though they may be action-oriented, as indeed I am, they creatively make time to read in their busy schedule. For me to keep up my discipline of reading a book a week, plus 12 journals, several popular magazines, and a daily newspaper, I use up five minutes here, and five minutes there throughout the day. A book is kept by my toilet, articles and journals in the back of my briefcase, and a book or two by my bedside. I actually keep about fifteen books on the go and finish an average of one a week. Large chunks of reading time are engaged in when I am flying and travelling long distances, all preplanned reading. That habit began as I bounced along in the back of a lorry overland to India from England, an arduous trip taking one whole month. It continued in my many days crisscrossing India on trains that took days to get anywhere.

Reading selectively is also important. While leaders perhaps should be somewhat eclectic in their reading habits, for the reasons cited above, they must also be well-read.[232] Quality and quantity go together in forming a sound reading discipline. As Gordon MacDonald exclaims: 'The ordering of our private world cannot take place without strong mental endurance and the intellectual growth this endurance produces.'[233] Moreover, a liberal education instead of narrowly-focused learning enables one to gain perspective on life.[234]

I use a highlighter pen to remember key thoughts and well-turned phrases. If I borrow a book, I get my secretary to type out the faintly earmarked sections so that I can keep a copy of the notes from the book in the appropriate file, by theme, before erasing the pencil marks in the book. Once I finish a book I will often review the highlighted sections in the book to help me retain and reflect on what I have read. About a quarter of my reading is for sheer relaxation and is secular in nature. The rest is divided between theology, devotional literature, commentaries, leadership, missiology, and church growth/ecclesiology.

A word in concluding this section is in order about learning in ways other than reading. The fact is that some people learn better through visual as opposed to verbal communication. Probing people's minds in pointed and deep conversation is stimulating and enlightening to some. My son learns best this way; he is very relational.[235] Then again, much of the emphasis in management

---

[232] Kenneth A. Myers has a fascinating analysis of C.S. Lewis on this subject in Chapter Six of his book *All God's Children and Blue Suede Shoes: Christians and Popular Culture* (Westchester, IL: Crossway Books, 1989).

[233] Gordon MacDonald, *Ordering Your Private World*, 90.

[234] Stephen Covey, *The 7 Habits of Highly Effective People*, 295.

[235] Robert Greenleaf claims the same preference to learn from conversation with others in *The Power of Servant Leadership*, 275.

literature in the way of knowledge capital, to be frank, has to do with keeping abreast of technological innovations. I'm not sure that that sort of learning relates readily to the type of leader we are talking about here, although developing know-how in any field is good for enhancing mental sharpness and versatility. Certainly today's generation of spiritual leaders needs to be computer-literate. However, their learning must help them to think broadly more than technically. Bennis and Nanus make this distinction too: 'Managers are usually well equipped to handle maintenance learning, but it is the leader's responsibility to ensure innovative learning.'[236]

Allow me to digress here slightly. I must confess a concern about the predilection of Generation X to learn by audio visual methods almost exclusively. Studies have shown that television (and we include videos and computer-based learning) is an extremely passive form of activity and hinders the ability to engage in conscious thought.[237] Brainwave activity is lessened considerably when a person watches television. It does not enhance coherency and intention in pursuing a train of thought in the way that written or oral interaction do, for example. Acquiring knowledge through images is different from doing so by words. Images communicate viscerally and intuitively whereas words communicate conceptually and abstractly. Images are subjectively processed while words are logically absorbed. Thus images affect moods while words present an argument.[238] Both aspects of

---

[236] Warren Bennis and Burt Nanus, *Leaders: The Strategies for Taking Charge*, 194.

[237] Leland Ryken, *Work and Leisure in Christian Perspective* (Portland, OR: Multnomah Press, 1987), 54.

[238] Kenneth A. Myers, *All God's Children and Blue Suede Shoes*, 162–163.

learning are valid and therefore needed. The danger for the Christian, and specifically of interest in this book, the Christian leader, is persuasively argued by Myers in these words: 'Images are wholly inadequate to express what ought to be, what ought not to be, or conditions under which something will or will not happen. In images, everything is in the present tense and the indicative mood. Images are very non-judgmental and undemanding. This poses some obvious problems for theology and ethics . . . One of the principal reasons for being literate is to be able to distinguish truth from falsehood. But if that distinction is regarded as less and less important in our lives, in politics, in art, in religion, then why bother learning to read?'[239]

Whatever way we learn, the servant leader perceives his or her self-development as a stewardship: without vitality the leader has failed watching followers. Thus Leighton Ford can say: 'Learning is the essential fuel for the leader. One way to recognize the true leader is this drive not only to learn, but to create what has been called a commonwealth of learning, an attitude and environment in which learning takes place.'[240]

Solitude

In one way of looking at it, the above disciplines are ones that provide solitude. Yet there is a kind of solitude that has rewards of its own, unrelated to having a quiet time and reading. It is what happens through an intentionalized removing of oneself from the common distractions of everyday life for a significant period of time. I am

---

[239] Ibid., 164, 168.
[240] Leighton Ford, *Transforming Leadership*, 212.

thinking of things that involve being alone without those cell phones and schedules for a day or more at a time. Such solitude can take different forms: prayer and fasting, going to a park or beach to get close to nature while you spend time with God reflectively, holing up in a hotel room with your Bible, a journal notebook, and some books, or spending several days at a retreat centre with a spiritual director interacting with you.

How important is solitude for the vitality of the servant leader? Willard maintains that 'solitude is the most radical of the disciplines for life in the spirit'.[241] He goes on to say this: 'In solitude we find the psychic distance, the perspective from which we can see, in the light of eternity, the created things that trap, worry, and oppress us.'[242] In this regard, it seems to play much the same function as observing the day of rest does. Pausing from the afflicting tyranny of the urgent of the day to day grind one day a week helps one to not take oneself too seriously as we catch a glimpse at that moment that the world has not stopped just because we have stopped. We see ourselves in perspective when we cease from our work, whether through observing a Sabbath or entering leisurely solitude, in other words.

It goes without saying that Jesus modelled this propensity for seeking solitude. He went into the wilderness to fast for 40 days (Mt. 4:1–11). He spent a whole night alone in prayer before choosing his twelve disciples (Luke 6:12; cf. Mt. 14:23; Mk. 1:35). After the adrenaline and adoration of a dramatic ministry event, *he withdrew by boat privately to a solitary place* (Mt. 14:13). He exhorted his disciples to rest away from the crowds after a hectic period of ministry (Mk. 6:31). He approached great tests by pursuing

---

[241] Dallas Willard, *The Spirit of the Disciplines*, 107.
[242] Ibid., 161.

solitude so he could pray undistractedly (Mt. 26:36–46).
Seeking of solitude was not an infrequent discipline of
his for it says in Luke 5:16 that 'Jesus often withdrew to
lonely places and prayed.'

What is the purpose of solitude? One only has to look at
how Jesus practised it to realize that it had to do with
'listening' to God. The noise of our contemporary world
mitigates against hearing that 'still small voice'. There is
the pursuit of solitude that comes from being a loner, from
being a social misfit. We are not advocating excessive
individualism. Community must also play a vital role in
sustaining and growing our spirituality. Bonhoeffer nicely
captures this distinction in this statement:

> Let him who cannot be alone beware of community . . . Let
> him who is not in community beware of being alone . . .
> Each by itself has profound pitfalls and perils. One who
> wants fellowship without solitude plunges into the void of
> words and feelings, and one who seeks solitude without
> fellowship perishes in the abyss of vanity, self-infatuation,
> and despair.[243]

Richard Foster would like to add the discipline of silence
to our discipline of solitude. He is quite right in distinguishing between them. Of course there is an external
silence imposed on oneself when you are canoeing on the
pristine waters of Algonquin Park, away from civiliza-
tion and all its noise pollution. God can and does speak
in a thundering voice in such quietness. Surely this is
what the prophet had in mind when he said that 'in
quietness and confidence is your strength' (Is. 30:15). But
sometimes we need to shut up and let God be discerned
in the silence before we pray. In such silence, not just

---

[243] Dietrich Bonhoeffer, *Life Together*, 77–78.

solitude, we feel like we stand before God and can see ourselves as he sees us, such is the palpable sense of being in his presence. And so we concur with Foster when he says,

> The tongue is our most powerful weapon of manipulation. A frantic stream of words flows from us because we are in a constant process of adjusting our public image. We fear so deeply what we think other people see in us, so we talk in order to straighten out their understanding . . . Silence is one of the deepest Disciplines of the Spirit simply because it puts a stopper on that. One of the fruits of silence is the freedom to let our justification rest entirely with God.[244]

Be that as it may, solitude can be used to take stock. At least once a year I take a day alone just to see if I am on target for fulfilling my life's mission, my short-term objectives, and to hear God speak in a special way. It has everything to do with stewardship: servant leaders monitor themselves to be sure they are not shortchanging those who are dependent on them for inspirational leadership. Thus it is not surprising to find that secular guru of servant leadership, Robert Greenleaf, claiming that 'as I have grown older, I have come to value solitude more and more'.[245] On the surface, withdrawing from others may seem the epitome of selfishness or narcissism, but in actuality it is necessary self-surgery.

On physical exercise

While not seeking to be a proponent of buffed bodies and buffoon minds, I risk being misunderstood in affirming

---

[244] Richard Foster, *Celebration of Discipline*, 88.
[245] Robert Greenleaf, *The Power of Servant Leadership*, 267.

the value of a certain measure of physical fitness in the individual who covets being a good servant leader. Over the years I have attended far too many leaders' meetings. I cannot help but see a correlation between those who have fallen asleep in those meetings and those who are slovenly physically. Their blood too easily rushed to their stomachs. While bodily exercise may profit little in relation to spiritual exercise, according to the apostle Paul, it is worth noting that he did not say that physical exercise was of no value! I repeat what I said at the end of my section on the importance of having a regular quiet time. All our faculties – mental, physical, emotional, and spiritual – need to be brought to bear on stimulating our vitality. Larry Richards has understood this principle in his book on spirituality, summarized nicely in this statement: 'Spirituality has to do with being an integrated person in the fullest sense.'[246] To associate the body (flesh) with evil inherently and the spirit alone as being good is to introduce a Greek dualism about the nature of the created order that is not found in Scripture and which has played havoc in the church in its longstanding dance of death around a secular/sacred bifurcation.

There are numerous clues in Scripture that our spiritual life is intricately connected with our mental and physical well-being. One thinks, for instance, of Elijah, whose depression was dealt with by the Lord, not by the imposition of a heavy dose of meditation and fasting, but by sleep and good food (1 Kings 19). Did not Christ, after fasting for forty days in the wilderness, seek to satisfy his hunger? Did he not interrupt ministry on more than one occasion to feed the crowds physically just as he had fed them spiritually? As I speak of physical exercise, I am

---

[246] Larry Richards, *A Practical Theology of Spirituality* (Grand Rapids, MI: Academie Books, 1987), 11.

also therefore thinking in terms of ministering to bodily needs in general. Sleep deprivation was the lot of the apostle Paul (2 Cor. 11:27) and it seems to be the lot of missionary executives too (speaking from personal experience). If not balanced by regular sleep routines and days off where possible, to compensate for jet lag and long working hours on the road, it exacts a deadly long term emotional toll. Hence Scripture gives us wise advice:

> Unless the LORD builds the house,
> its builders labour in vain.
> Unless the LORD watches over the city,
> the watchmen stand guard in vain.
> In vain you rise early
> and stay up late,
> toiling for food to eat –
> for he grants sleep to those he loves. (Psalm 127:1,2)

Elsewhere we are exhorted to *honour God with our bodies* (1 Cor. 6:19–20). Surely running guru George Sheenan was right in saying that we have four roles we need to constantly improve in: being a good animal (physical), a good craftsman (mental), a good friend (social), and a saint (spiritual).[247] Neglect of any one of these areas, I would contend, saps us of our full vitality as humans made in God's image.

We have become a sedentary society and yet the body has not been built for physical inactivity.[248] Most medical authorities agree that we must exercise at least three times a week with our heart rate increased to eighty per

---

[247] Cited in Stephen Covey, *First Things First*.
[248] Richard E. Ecker, *Staying Well: Why the Good Life Is So Bad for Your Health* (Downer's Grove, IL: InterVarsity Press, 1984), 83.

cent of capacity for a minimum of twenty minutes at a time in order to give a sufficient workout to the cardio-vascular system so as to avoid heart disease later in life.[249] For me that is primarily done through running; for others it may be squash, aerobics, canoeing, or swimming. For certain individuals reading this book, the best way they can grow as servant leaders is to overcome their progression toward couch potato status. The worst thing some of you can do is to relax by watching TV. Varying stresses can be good. Sure you have faced a day of pressurized mental and emotional stresses, but to contrast that with a physical workout would actually revitalize rather than further drain you. To discipline yourself in working up a decent sweat is to give yourself just the sort of emotional reward that you feel you deserve after a hard day's work at a desk but which you instead give yourself by over indulging in your eating or by plopping yourself down in front of that TV set.

Along with exercise, of course, is the question of diet. It is far easier to gain weight by eating than by failing to exercise. Do you realize how many hours of jogging it takes to burn off the calories found in a strawberry short-cake dessert? Really, the two must go together: healthy eating and diligent exercising. If you do not enjoy exercising alone, join a sports team. This past summer at the age of 51 I joined a softball team and had a great time. Team sports can also lead to tremendous witnessing opportunities. In fact one of the young adults playing on our team has started coming to our church and has accepted Christ as Saviour, and now her older sister has, too. Anyhow, moderation in food intake and a lifestyle that includes a steady dose of physical exercise is God-honouring and revitalizing.

---

[249] Ibid., 88.

On holidays and enjoying the day of rest

In our society's obsession with time management, we have lost the capacity to keep perspective on our lives. A few minutes shaved off a task here and a few hours saved by ingenuity there have shaped us to be *chronos* giants but *kairos* dwarfs.[250] Failure to build in quality 'down time' to our weekly schedules has left us without adequate perspective on our lives, broken marriages, wayward children, and spiritual impoverishment.

In the Protestant concern to avoid legalism at all costs, we have perhaps overreacted in neglecting spiritual disciplines which Roman Catholics have adhered to across the centuries, and which were part of the fabric of the early church. Arguing that the one commandment not reinforced in the NT is the honouring of the Sabbath Rest, evangelicals have tended to downplay the value of doing more than worship on the Sabbath – now observed, of course, except for Seventh Day Adventists, on the first day of the week, coinciding with Christ's resurrection. Puritan observance of the Lord's Day in a very fastidious manner is often cited as being a grace killer and therefore inappropriate practice for those living in the age of grace. Therefore, it is not abnormal to find believers working on Sundays when they have a choice not to, to shop in malls to their hearts' content, and to do every kind of work under the sun around the house.[251] Sunday is just like any other day – except that believers worship at church for

---

[250] Stephen Covey develops this distinction thoroughly in his book *First Things First*.

[251] It needs to be acknowledged, nevertheless, that some jobs require a seven days a week commitment – like nursing, and policing. The spirit and not the letter of the law should be adhered to in such cases.

the first part of the day (now reduced from morning and evening services to just morning!).

To our harm, we have failed to forge a theology of rest that factors in the simple realization that the principle of ceasing from work is built into creation; it is more than one of the ten commandments. Therefore to presuppose that honouring the one-day-in-seven rest principle is from the OT law and hence non-binding, is incorrect. Repeatedly, the injunction issued to God's people to rest and worship on the seventh day is predicated on the example of God doing so in the process of creation (e.g. Gen. 2:1–3; Ex. 20:8–11; 31:17). The Deuteronomic version of the commandment to rest is different from its form in Exodus. In the later version the rationale for observing it is to remember God's redemption of his people from Egypt (Deut. 5:12–15). Worth noting here is that the Sabbath commandment is the only one that appears in two different forms in the two versions of the ten commandments in Scripture. At any rate, it could be argued that both for creation reasons and for celebratory reasons, the commandment should not be jettisoned in the age of the church. In other words, the principle to practise is both to worship as a community of believers and to rest from normal labours on one day of the week (Num. 28:18,25,26).

Pragmatically, my opinion is that we cannot afford to live without the day of rest and worship. Without getting into the subject of how some spiritual refreshment and growth fail to occur in isolation from the community of a local church, looking at the rest dimension alone with respect to the observance of the Lord's Day, there is much to commend it. Since I have made a greater effort to make one day in seven special in the sense of not doing normal work on it (Sunday is not the pastor's day of rest incidentally), I have noticed that my blood pressure has lowered, I enjoy greater stamina when I am working, my productivity at work has improved, I don't take myself so seriously, my marriage has improved, and I enjoy the Lord and his service more. Leland Ryken is absolutely spot on in the following observations.

> The spirit of self-denial and asceticism (rejecting earthly pleasures as evil) has run strong in the Christian tradition. So has the sense of duty. I do not wish to deny that self-denial and duty are necessary parts of the Christian life. But they are not the whole of the Christian life. When carried away beyond their legitimate place, they end up robbing the Christian life of the joy that should accompany it . . .
>
> Work and leisure take their meaning from each other. Without leisure, work narrows life down and damages the worker. But leisure by itself also robs a person of fulness. Without work, people feel useless and lack sufficient purpose in life.[252]

One of the things identified above by way of an insight gained from following the rhythm of six days of working followed by one day of resting followed again by the six days of working is that it helps us to keep our earthly contribution (to work or ministry) in perspective. As Dorothy Bass articulates: 'To act as if the world cannot get along without our work for one day in seven is a startling display of pride that denies the sufficiency of our generous Maker . . . Refraining from work on a regular basis should also teach us not to demand excessive work from others . . . Sabbath affirms the value of work and interprets it as an important dimension of human identity.'[253]

Even secular sources attribute value to the development of a weekly rhythm that includes sufficient rest to cope

---

[252] Leland Ryken, *Work and Leisure in Christian Perspective*, 191, 262.
[253] Dorothy C. Bass, "Rediscovering the Sabbath', *Christianity Today* (September 1, 1997), 43.

with the rigours of a dog eat dog world. Witness the words of Covey: 'The week represents a complete patch in the fabric of life. It has workdays, evenings, the weekend ... The week provides us with three useful operating perspectives: 1) balanced renewal, 2) whole-parts-whole, and 3) content in context. The perspective of the week prompts us to plan for renewal – a time for recreation and reflection – weekly and daily.'[254]

For me, in full-time pastoral ministry, it is imperative that I contrast my day off activities with what I do otherwise on a daily basis. By comparison, those who do not have the luxury of studying God's word by the hour on a typical day, as I do, or of visiting with a senior living alone, or mapping out the church's future at a board meeting, they will want to take more time on their day of rest to reflect on the deep things of God, perhaps picking up a devotional classic like *Pilgrim's Progress* on a quiet Sunday afternoon or visiting a sick church member in hospital. But I will forego such things as much as possible (except for my quiet time) on my day off – instead, golfing, doing household chores that I find liberating after a week of desk and devotional duty, and leisurely pursuits with my wife. (For example, visiting the McMichael Collection of Canada's famous Group of Seven painters, preceded by a delightful lunch in an intimate restaurant in the quaint town where the McMichael Collection is exhibited.) Then again that day off might mean driving a couple of hours to where my son lives and helping him renovate his first house (much as I am not much of a handy man around the house!). The point is that the day of rest is meant to provide a contrast to the six days of work we otherwise face week after week. I must confess that in the 'unspiritual' activity of pottering around the

---

[254] Stephen Covey, *First Things First*, 156.

house (a luxury I don't afford myself six days of the week) or on the golf course with the ball leaving a trail on the dew-drenched fairway, I sometimes experience my epiphanies. Those unexpected encounters with God can renew me as much as a month of quiet times.

Gordon MacDonald wonderfully compares the result of observing this day of rest on a weekly basis to the effect of 'repounding' New England clapboards which come loose through the expanding and contracting of seasonal temperature changes.[255] The Sabbath discipline recalibrates the spirit just as occasional repounding of clapboards keeps the house from losing its walls.

How we are to spend our day of rest is unique for each one of us. For instance, for a farmer to work in his vegetable plot and flower garden next to his house on a Sunday afternoon is not going to be relaxing and non-work in the way it may be for the computer operator in a high rise office tower. But we do need to avoid the subtleties of rationalization that a consumer and success-driven world impose on our psyche so as to justify our continuing in just another form of work as we struggle with this idea of resting, thus missing the blessing of truly practising the Sabbath.[256]

In addition to those days off on a regular basis, we need lengthier periods of time to refreshen our body, soul, and spirit. There are Christian leaders I know who do not have holidays, beyond, perhaps, an extended weekend, wearing this notoriety almost like a badge of honour. There seem to be two extremes among those who

---

[255] Gordon MacDonald, *Ordering Your Private World*, 168.

[256] Not to be ignored too, is our tendency as evangelicals to cram Sunday full of so many church activities that it becomes anything but a day of rest. Pastors and Christian leaders must watchfully exercise integrity with their people in this area and not demand too much of them on that day.

make their living by the gospel; a tendency to be lazy, or to be workaholics.[257] Of particular concern for us at this juncture is the latter group of people who are over-achievers. That this Sabbath rest is a biblical concept is evident from the number of special days (Num. 28:18,25,26), weeks (Neh. 8:14–18), and even years (Lev. 25) the Israelites were to set aside to worship the Lord and to cease from their labours. The balance between the two is seen, for example, in Ecclesiastes 2:24: 'A man can do nothing better than to eat and drink and find satisfaction in his work.'

A good theology of work necessitates an aside on the theology of leisure.[258] Suffice it to say here that the way God designed us requires a variety of measures taken to accomplish the desired goal of revitalization. What holidays achieve that the day of rest cannot is an ability to fully unwind and relax from the pressures of our vocation and the frenetic pace of life in the postmodern world. Furthermore, they enable us to catch up on the family! One of my favourite childhood memories is of an extended camping trip my father made with the four oldest children in our family. As we went tenting from one provincial park to another on the Canadian side of Lake Huron, Lake Ontario, and Lake Erie, we not only stored up precious memories of spectacular nature scenes but of bonding with our father in ways that his busy life normally prevented us from doing.

The etymology of the word *leisure* suggests 'free time', the kind we associate with non-work. One of the term's roots is *lesir* meaning 'to be allowed or to be

---

[257] Phil Parshall, 'Why Some People Are Unproductive', *Evangelical Missions Quarterly* (June 1990), 246–251.
[258] For an extended coverage of these two subjects from a biblical perspective I recommend Leland Ryken, *Work and Leisure in Christian Perspective*.

lawful'.[259] The key idea is liberty to do something, captured in a word deriving from it, *license*. The other root word is from the Greek *skole* from which we derive the word *school*. Originally the word conveyed the idea of 'halting or ceasing' and came to mean having spare time for oneself and hence for one's self-development. And so we come to see how our contemporary usage of leisure relates to this sense of unforced use of time.

Let's face it. There are some things we crave doing which a Sabbath just does not allow time for. That may include engaging in extensive renovations or painting projects around the house that otherwise never seem to get done. While a certain aspect of home improvement projects may hardly seem like unforced activity, there is a sense in which any physical labour for those whose vocation is primarily cerebral or relational is very freeing and therapeutic.[260] However, one person's leisure may be another person's work. The point is that holidays permit you the luxury of doing things or being a certain way that you are normally unable to. For example, it may be to give yourself passionately to your hobby. It is worth noting that many great figures of church history had hobbies. William Carey, for instance, was known for his fascination with botany, forestry, and biology. After settling at Serampore, he fashioned a five acre garden which within a few years became one of the finest botanical collections in Asia.[261] Out of his hobby, which he pursued avidly until

---

[259] Ibid., 29.

[260] Paul Stevens has an interesting discussion in his book, *Liberating the Laity*, on the profound lessons he learned from leaving 'full-time' ministry for carpentry and construction work for a period of time.

[261] Kellsye M. Finnie, *William Carey: By Trade A Cobbler* (Eastbourne, UK: Kingsway Publications, 1986), 147.

shortly before his death, was born the Horticultural and Agricultural Society of India. It was the famous British doctor, William Osler, who reputedly remarked, 'No man is happy without a hobby and it makes precious little difference what outside interest it might be . . . anything, as long as he straddles a hobby and rides it hard.'

In summary, we echo the words of Ryken about the value of leisure as being essential to the rhythms of life that lead to revitalization: 'Leisure is not ethically neutral. It flourishes only when people believe in the goodness of pleasure and human fulfillment. It withers when people are lazy, preoccupied with what is useful, or given to self-denial.'[262]

Conclusion

Consider the maintenance of personal vitality for the leader as being akin to re-potting of plants.[263] My wife and I have a Christmas cactus that has followed us around from house to house wherever we have moved. It is a fixture in our home. Our Christmas cactus is almost as old as our marriage. Every once in a while it needs to be re-potted because its roots have outgrown its present abode and it has begun to avoid blossoming on schedule or sprout new offshoots of greenery when it should. Such is what happens when we take our walk with the Lord for granted or when we treat the calling of leadership as other than the sacred stewardship it entails.

Perhaps you are one of those whom I know will read this chapter and feel guilty rather than stimulated, drained

---

[262] Ibid., 40.
[263] H.B. London and Neil B. Wiseman, *The Heart of a Great Pastor*, 43.

rather than revitalized. I have just added five more 'thou shalt nots' and five more 'to dos' to your burdensome list. Let me then close with the words of Fred Smith, ones I feel are appropriate if you find yourself intimidated by this proposed dimension of servant leadership.

Finally, many people approach self-development as one more thing they ought to do, whether they want to or not. Not doing it makes them feel guilty.

Forcing yourself to do something you dislike is ultimately dangerous, like running a motor without oil: You build up heat, build up tension, and eventually destroy the motor.

The secret of growing for a lifetime is to move from seeing self-development as a burden to seeing it as a joy – the way to fulfill responsibility, the path of worthwhile accomplishment. Once it becomes that, we will automatically do it, for we do the things we enjoy.[264]

---

[264] Fred Smith, 'Training To Reach the Top', *Leadership* (Spring 1996), 39.

7

Teachability: You can always learn something new

Although similar to *vitality*, we treat *teachability* as a trait of the servant leader distinguishable from vitality because of a discernibly different attitude that lies behind it. Vitality recognizes that muscles, whether spiritual, mental, or physical, need exercise in order to avoid atrophy: teachability recognizes that it is easy to overestimate how developed our muscles really are. Vitality has more to do with acquiring knowledge, teachability with acquiring wisdom. There is a humility engendered in teachability that may be missing in vitality. Bertrand Russell brimmed with intellectual luminosity but that did not necessarily mean that he was morally sharp. This trait of teachability is discernible in the leader who keeps improving in areas he or she is already strong in, who resists the temptation to assume self-perception is the same as others' perception of them, and who accepts the value of conflict because of personal lessons that can be learned from it.

Not resting on one's laurels

Too many of us are legends in our own minds. That self-confidence brought ancient Troy to ruins. It is the

Achilles heel of many a Christian leader. We start to believe our own press releases. Before we know it, we are running on the exhaust fumes of the deference and adulation people pay us as they see God at work (or so they think) through us. It becomes ever so easy to use 'God talk' to reinforce this invincibility as Cheryl Forbes so incisively documents in her probing book, *Religion of Power*.[265] Who can argue with *God has revealed to me* or *It is God's will* or *I prayed about it* in order to justify a course of action taken as a leader? In other words, 'church' language is sometimes used to get our own way but in fact we spiritualize this manipulation without others realizing it. Before we know it, we ourselves no longer distinguish between our own will and God's will. Pretty soon we start believing that we can make no mistakes, that we have a special anointing that overshadows the ministry and wishes of our colleagues, and that we have nothing more to learn spiritually. This was King Saul's fatal flaw. In setting his own terms as God's leader, he became presumptuous and so fell long and far.

This attitude of conceit reveals itself in different ways, one of which is to permit oneself the luxury of mental laziness. Instead of at a minimum seeking to grow in the areas we know we are gifted in already, so as to become even more effective, we show no interest in listening or looking. Covey identifies this close-mindedness well when he exhorts,

> Most of our mental development and study discipline comes through formal education. But as soon as we leave the external discipline of school, many of us let our minds atrophy. We don't do any more serious reading, we don't explore new subjects in any real depth outside our action

---

[265] Cheryl Forbes, *The Religion of Power* (Bromley, UK: MARC, 1986).

fields, we don't think analytically, we don't write – at least not critically or in a way that tests our ability to express ourselves in distilled, clear, and concise language. Instead, we spend our time watching TV.[266]

Winston Churchill was sixty-six before he became prime minister. Moses spent forty years in the wilderness before he was qualified to lead the children of Israel. Paul spent 14 years in obscurity after his conversion while he got his act together. Even Jesus, the Son of God in the flesh, did not enter his public ministry until the age of thirty: he only spent about nine per cent of his life in the public domain. All these examples considered, a dose of humility is fitting as we consider our preparedness for leadership. We should have the mindset that accepts that we never arrive but are always in a state of perpetual growing and improving. This is what John Gardener had in mind in the following statement in his classic book on leadership: 'Leadership development is a process that extends over many years. The realities of life require (and justify) selection and training that occur early in the individual's career, but that is only a first step. Leadership development calls for repeated assessments and repeated opportunities for training.'[267]

A deep impression was made on me when I discovered in the course of completing my Doctor of Ministry degree at Gordon-Conwell Theological Seminary near Boston that I would be required to see a psychologist and take a MBTI test before I could graduate. To someone twenty years into full-time ministry, this navel-gazing seemed to be somewhat superfluous and I went reluctantly. However, that hour with the psychologist going over the results of my test was most enlightening and helped me to see

[266] Stephen Covey, *The 7 Habits of Highly Effective People*, 294–295.
[267] John Gardener, *On Leadership*, 171.

myself more objectively. The psychologist's observations explained some of the reactions I had had in working with my colleagues over the years. I saw weaknesses in my leadership that I had never seen before. It was a good object lesson to me of the value of remaining teachable.

How often I have oriented new missionaries in candidate training about the importance of their being *FAT*: *F*lexible, *A*vailable, and *T*eachable. The trouble is that you do not learn this once and for all. It is not consummated by that character formation of the first term of service on the mission field. It is not finished by that baptism of fire of your first pastorate. Nor of your first leadership experience. Given that we have a fallen nature, and that we are in a spiritual warfare, we can be assured that our self-perception is myopic enough to take us a lifetime to overcome. The battle for self-objectivity is life-long.

Bobby Clinton speaks of convergence when it comes to shaping leaders. Convergence, according to him, occurs later in our career when we have acquired the skill set of understanding and putting to use effectively our unique blend of spiritual gifts, and gained the experience of learned lessons in godliness. Summing up this thesis, he says, 'God develops a leader over a lifetime. That development is a function of the use of events and people to impress leadership lessons upon a leader, time, and leader response.'[268]

One gets this sense of continual striving for improvement and of a teachable spirit in the advice Paul gives the young leader Timothy toward the end of Paul's life of service, when he exhorts: 'In the presence of God and of Christ Jesus . . . I give you this charge: preach the Word; be prepared in season and out of season; correct, rebuke and encourage – with great patience and careful instruction . . . But you,

---

[268] Bobby Clinton, *The Making of a Leader*, 25.

keep your head in all situations, endure hardship, do the work of an evangelist, discharge all the duties of your ministry' (2 Timothy 4:1–5). There is in these words the challenge to a pursuit of a life of excellence in service that does not involve taking the path of least resistance. Such is the attitude of the servant leader. The servant leader pushes for greater fruitfulness and is not satisfied for other than the Lord's 'well done, good and faithful servant' (Matt. 25:21). She or he will do whatever it takes to keep growing, to keep sharpening those skills required in order to be a good leader.

We have already addressed the issue of not resting on one's laurels, in one sense, by what we had to say in the last chapter about revitalization. Teachability also came across as a quality of servant leadership when we talked about the leader being able to admit weakness and being open to criticism (in the chapter on vulnerability). But there is a self-scrutiny that Scripture encourages that goes beyond these things. Paul says, for instance, to 'examine yourselves to see whether you are in the faith; test yourselves' (2 Cor. 13:5a). We talked in Chapter Two about understanding your intrinsic leadership style and of how your leadership style needs to be adjusted according to the context within which you must exercise leadership. That situational leadership is not going to be possible for the leader who is not able to critique his or her own self objectively enough. As Hershey and Blanchard have made clear in their ground-breaking book which introduced the Tri-Dimensional Leader Effectiveness Model, not only is the leader's self-perception of style (of how he or she is perceived by the followers) important in functioning as a leader, but understanding how your followers perceive you is also a weighty factor in deciding how to lead.[269]

---

[269] Paul Hershey and Kenneth Blanchard, *Management of Organizational Behavior*, 128–133.

Part of the situation in which you lead, then, includes what your employees or colleagues think about you, what style of leadership is appropriate in relating to them, etc. The behaviour pattern that a person exhibits in trying to impact the activities of others may be perceived differently by the two parties. To the extent that a leader squares his or her self-perception with that which the group has of him or her, the more effective will be the leadership.

To bridge that gap in self-knowledge (not that the group always has a correct assessment of the leader's character and intentions and style), a teachable spirit is crucial. That humility is formed in several ways. Just as breast cancer can be pre-empted (or caught early) by self-examination, so character flaws and shortcomings in one's leadership style can be overcome with perpetual self-examination. Brouwer understood this well, as indicated by his article, which is now considered as a classic by Harvard Business School. He says, 'The function of self-examination is to lay the groundwork for insight, without which no growth can occur ... Real, genuine glimpses of ourselves as we really are are reached only with difficulty and sometimes real psychic pain. Thus they are the building blocks of growth.'[270]

The ability not to take oneself too seriously found in true servant leaders ushers in teachability. It enables one to take a hard look at oneself on a regular basis, kind of like having a placard hanging around your neck which says WORK IN PROGRESS and which you are forced to notice every once in a while. Peter Drucker puts it this way in listing six things all effective leaders he knows do: 'One way or another they submitted themselves to the *"mirror test"* – that is, they made sure that the person they saw in the

---

[270] Paul Brouwer, 'The Power To See Ourselves', 40.

mirror in the morning was the kind of person they wanted to be, respect, and believe in. This way they fortified themselves against the leader's greatest temptations – to do things that are popular rather than right and to do petty, mean, and sleazy things.'[271]

Being married presents the unique opportunity to get some free advice! Some spouses are quite free with the criticism, as people like John Wesley and William Carey discovered, to their chagrin. Others, like my own, are discreet, and reluctant to crush their spouse's delicate ego. Nonetheless, ask your husband or your wife for an honest opinion. About how you come across to the audience in your preaching. About whether your efforts at motivating co-workers are perceived by them as inspirational envisioning or manipulative flattery. About whether your hyper-activity makes you appear significant or a poor planner in the eyes of your colleagues. Insight borne of a new perception can lead to changing self-expectations to changing behaviour to better performance.

Our uncanny knack of misreading our usefulness to the Lord – of how others respond to us, in effect – is abundantly made clear to me when it comes to my preaching. Many times I step into the pulpit feeling that I have nothing really prophetic to say, that I do not have God's anointing in any special way, only to have more positive feedback than usual from some in the congregation afterwards. When someone at the church door tells me, 'After what you said this morning about money management, pastor, I know the Lord was speaking directly to me, and I have to go home right away and make some changes', you know that you were misled by your feelings when you felt nothing special earlier on

---

[271] Peter Drucker, 'Your Leadership Is Unique', *Leadership* (Fall 1996), 55.

stepping into the pulpit. Other times I have had the experience that I thought the message was delivered very smoothly, was full of brilliant illustrations, and people seemed to be paying attention, only to have absolutely no one compliment me on the sermon afterwards. How little we really know ourselves, as preaching constantly reminds me. The prophet Jeremiah put it this way: 'The heart is deceitful above all things and beyond cure. Who can understand it?' (Jer. 17:9).

Theologically, given that fallenness which Jeremiah underscored, we ought to be in a position to develop a healthy distrust of ourselves. Furthermore, evidence of the conflicts we have with people as we lead them should only reinforce that scepticism of the accuracy of our self-perception. Now scientists, particularly psychologists, are finding a whole series of flaws in the ways we think in making decisions, from biases due to faulty thinking, to conditioning based on traumatic childhood experiences. In a brilliant article Hammond, Keeney, and Raiffa, management consultants, identify four faulty thinking traps, which the leader must be cognizant of within him or herself, in order to lead effectively.[272]

- *The Anchoring Trap:* When contemplating a decision, the mind gives disproportionate weight to the first information it receives. We all know from embarrassing experience how we have subsequently not allowed the facts to disturb our first impressions of someone. Ways leaders can compensate for the unconscious tendency for this heuristic habit to kick in include always viewing a problem from different angles, pre-empting the advice

---

[272] John S. Hammond, Ralph L. Keeney, and Howard Raiffa, 'The Hidden Traps in Decision Making', *Harvard Business Review* (September/October 1998), 47–58.

of those around you by thinking about the problem on your own first, and seeking a wide range of advice.

- *The Status Quo Trap:* Advice that perpetuates the status quo is disproportionately accepted. The more choices you have in making a decision, for example, the more likely you are to settle for the status quo. Always remember when trying to compensate for this habit of the mind that the desirability of the status quo changes over time. Force yourself to choose between better alternatives rather than just falling back on the familiar just because that is the easier way out.

- *The Sunk-Cost Trap:* This trap likes justifying past behaviour or choices. How especially true this habit is when it comes to people: we defend a colleague we have hired or discipled long after it is evident that this co-worker is not worth keeping or relying on. To compensate for this trap, try consulting people who have nothing invested in the relationship while deciding what to do about this difficult colleague. Office politics (or church politics) can muddy the waters far too easily. Be able to admit your error in judgment. A little bit of humility never hurt any leader!

- *The Confirming-Evidence Trap:* This bias seeks out information or points of view that confirm our preference while being impervious to alternative perspectives. An inclination to be more engaged by things we like than we dislike is a similar habit, of which we may be far from conscious. For instance, I prefer sermon preparation to visitation of the elderly and that may affect my decisions on time usage as a pastor more than I would care to admit. How do you deal with this tendency? Well, for one thing, you can have friends who serve as Job's Comforters in keeping you accountable. Moreover, in seeking the advice of others, do not ask leading questions that invite predictable responses.

- *The Framing Trap:* This trap basically reckons with the fact that the way we frame the question about the problem or the decision to be made affects the choices that are made. A recognition of this problem explains why doctoral thesis advisors in the academic setting can be tigers when it comes to the approving of the framing of the student's thesis question, but be pussy cats when it comes to actually evaluating the thesis proper. They have understood that objectivity and therefore accurate findings are mutually inclusive!

What are other ways to plot strategies against your inherent fallenness? One is to get into an accountability group. I have built into my lifestyle this habit of being accountable to someone or some group. I prefer to be in a group or a relationship that is so structured that all areas of life are gradually covered over the course of many meetings. Moreover, accountability sessions should be structured with a series of barbed or pointed questions that do not allow much 'squirm' room. Questions that address the thought life, the state of one's marriage, the use of leisure time . . . and 'the big three' of money, sex, and power. Wherever possible, my accountability regimen includes using Gordon MacDonald's comprehensive set of accountability questions.[273]

Objective self-knowledge takes a lifetime of learning and that is why we cannot rest on our laurels as leaders. While developing skill sets is relevant to leadership development, developing character is relevant to servant leadership, the kind of distinction in emphasis Covey goes to great trouble to make in *Principle-Centered Leadership*. Objective self-knowledge is likewise considered in Scripture to be a weightier matter. Thus in the chapter on spiritual gifts,

---

[273] Gordon MacDonald, *Rebuilding Your Broken World*, 230–231.

Romans 12, Paul adds this word of caution to those who would be swept away by their own charisma: 'Do not think of yourself more highly than you ought, but rather think of yourself with sober judgment, in accordance with the measure of faith God has given you' (v. 3). As we probe our motives in alert self-reflection, we must allow the word of God to act like a mirror for us, and use various methods to understand ourselves more accurately, disciplines that can only help us to become better leaders. In becoming better leaders, we, in turn, are helping those who follow us, and that spells *servanthood*. Brouwer says it well: 'If the proposition is right that realism in the individual's view of himself has a one-to-one relationship with effectiveness on the job, then it surely follows that all of us can improve our effectiveness by the simple expedient of developing a more realistic, more accurate self-concept!'[274]

What are some of the specific benefits to our leadership that come out of constructive introspection? If such insight leads to understanding ourselves better, it may mean, for example, that we explode the myths we might have built up over the years about what our real strengths are. Speaking personally, in my early years of leadership, I had a distorted view of my own relational abilities. In fact I score quite low on the people-friendly side of leadership styles.[275] Coming to grips with that fact is what kept me from the pastoral ministry and in mission executive leadership longer than I otherwise might have

---

[274] Paul Brouwer, 'The Power To See Ourselves', 39.

[275] As measured by the Rowe and Mason Decision Style Inventory, mentioned in Chapter One. Their four quadrants are *directive, analytical, conceptual*, and *behavioural*. It is this latter quadrant that I am referring to above and which is the most pastoral of the four quadrants.

stayed. Later, another breakthrough emerged, which actually had the opposite effect, of freeing me to consider becoming a pastor. That insight into myself was to see that I was trying too much to be all things to all people. In actual fact, I needed to realize that all the strengths needed in pastors – ability to teach the word powerfully and clearly, organizational savvy, a shepherd's heart to comfort and help the emotionally and spiritually wounded, mentoring and discipling skills, to name but the main ones – did not all have to reside in one person. In fact the leader or the church that expects a pastor to meet all these qualifications is setting itself up for a fall and is likely to be dysfunctional. A church putting all their hopes for growth in the pastor will either develop unrealistic expectations of him or her, or be too dependent on the pastor. Therefore, as I took my first pastorate, I was up-front with the board in telling them what areas of ministry I felt I was weak in, and also in challenging them to think of the pastoral leadership in the church as a team effort. They hired me and subsequently agreed to bringing in an associate pastor whom I felt had strengths that complemented mine. Between the two of us, then, we felt that we could, with the help of the elders, attend to our various duties and responsibilities effectively. My current church has a healthy view of the importance of team leadership and so my leadership style is relatively a non-issue.

If it is true that we tend to know better what we are not good at than what we are good at, and yet that we can only effectively minister from our strengths, then servant leadership requires that we get in touch with our strengths too.[276] Peter Drucker maintains that the only way to adequately discover your strengths is through feedback

---

[276] Peter Drucker, 'Managing Oneself', 66.

analysis – such as is engaged in by writing down your expectations when you make a key decision or take a key action and then comparing the actual results with your expectations months later.[277]

He also encourages working on those strengths. His thinking fits congruently with the point I am trying to make in this section when he urges: 'Discover where your intellectual arrogance is causing disabling ignorance and overcome it. Far too many people – especially people with great expertise in one area – are contemptuous of knowledge in other areas or believe that being bright is a substitute for knowledge'.[278] If you have been called to be a cross-cultural communicator of the gospel, and have already learned well the language of the people you are reaching, do not assume that you are contextualizng your message adequately, but do further reading in anthropology and missiology to sharpen your contextualizing ability. Also, find ways to immerse yourself in the host culture more.

If you are a pastor with a grasp of how churches grow and possess a track record of seeing churches blossom in growth, keep sharpening that anointing by visiting churches that are exponentially growing, to gain further insights, and continue to read widely in practical theology and ecclesiology. The type of stewardship we are envisioning here whereby one is not resting on one's laurels and is thus remaining teachable is summarized well by Drucker again: 'One should waste as little effort as possible on improving areas of low competence. It takes far more energy and work to improve from incompetence to mediocrity than it takes to improve from first-rate performance to excellence.'[279]

---

[277] Ibid.
[278] Ibid.
[279] Ibid., 67.

Some essential insights to come to about oneself as a leader include: Do I work best in management or as an executive leader? As a senior pastor or as an associate pastor? As a church planter in missions or in a support role? How easy it is to perpetuate the 'Peter Principle' of rising to one's level of incompetence. Know your limits and live within them. Do you communicate best one-on-one or in public settings? By writing or by speaking? Do you do cerebral work better in the morning or the evening? Are you energized by being around people or by being alone? Do you perform best under pressure and stress or do you need to plan and prioritize so as to minimize the number of occasions when you find yourself in that situation? The way you answer such questions, and more importantly, make time management plans on the basis of this knowledge, will determine your effectiveness as a leader, in large measure. In concluding the examination of the principle outlined in this section, we could not do better than to remind ourselves of the words of Micah: 'He has showed you, O man, what is good. And what does the LORD require of you? To act justly, and to love mercy, and *to walk humbly with your God'* (6:8).[280] After all, in the face of Satan's commitment to deceive us (2 Cor. 11:3) and of our total depravity (Rom.7:21–25) so as to conspire to keep us proud, that is, having an exaggerated or distorted view of what we really are like or capable of performing, objective self-knowledge is not easy to come by. Humility is what God is looking for and what was so characteristic of his Son when he walked on this earth. The Christ's gentle and humble nature we are to emulate and to embrace (Phil. 2:1–8).

---

[280] Emphasis mine.

Turning conflict to your own advantage

We are not talking here about one-upmanship. About always having a winner and a loser in a conflict. We are considering how to learn positive lessons from false accusations. About how to find the kernel of truth in a personality conflict that reveals more about your antagonist's background and psychological makeup than your own faults. Teachability is one thing when you are the one to blame in a conflict but quite something else when you are *not* the main cause of the tension.

I hesitate to be anecdotal at this juncture for fear of causing speculation about whom I am talking, so I will only refer to an interpersonal conflict where the other party is now dead. For two years while I was on a mass evangelism team with OM in India I experienced the statistical oddity – but no doubt God-ordained coincidence – of having the same Indian national serve with me on the same team in spite of the constant reconfiguration of OM's evangelism teams around India totalling 250 different people. At one point, this brother was one of only two people serving on the team with me (normally we had about ten members on a team) as we departed from our usual work and did the groundwork in planning for a large scale evangelistic outreach. The problem was that this brother was impossible to live with. At first, I dismissed it as a personality clash. Then I thought that it was a clash of cultures and since I was the foreigner, the onus was on me to walk the extra mile. Many years later I learned two things about him: one was that no team wanted him to serve with it (OM had about 25 evangelism teams in India). The other was that he regularly beat his wife and had lost his testimony (I had preached at his wedding curiously enough). However, one side of me always refused to justify my persistent animosity toward him. I realized that his provoking habit of questioning my every decision (I was the team leader) was somehow refining that very tendency in me to be lacking in submission to authority figures. I was vaguely in touch with knowing that sublimation was going on, that is, that I was reacting to the qualities I saw in him that needed to be adjusted and sanctified within myself. In learning to love the unlovable, I was able to make headway in spiritual formation that needed to occur within myself.

Earlier, I cited the story of Italian Franco Bernabe, who rocketed to power as CEO of ENI, Italy's massive, energy-based industrial corporation. He took ENI through a very turbulent transition in his six year tenure as CEO during which time he also faced personal attack. He was accused of taking a bribe in spite of his scrupulosity about integrity in such matters. As Bernabe recalled his reaction to seeing this news on TV for the first time, that reaction is germane to what we are talking about with regard to turning negative criticism into a learning opportunity.

Bernabe immediately after receiving this devastating news went for a long walk and thought, 'This kind of attack is why I am fighting [to save ENI], and I will keep fighting even harder now. And if they think I will go away, they are wrong. Before I am finished, they will all be left behind, the people who think they can control ENI with politics and rumors and lies.'[281] He was prepared to add a new dimension to his leadership, in other words, courageously facing a sophisticated form of opposition, instead of taking the path of least resistance by resigning.

---

[281] Linda Hill and Suzy Wetlaufer, 'Leadership When There Is No One To Ask: An Interview with ENI's Franco Bernabe', 85–6.

That this teachability under fire was not an accident, to me, is made apparent later in the interview, when Bernabe describes how he walked to work every day to allow time for critical thinking: 'I must say,' he muses, 'I did not "react" during the crisis. I always thought things through – I very carefully went through all the problems I had, analyzing them from every angle. Why do you think I walk to work every day? It gives me an extra half hour to think. Strategic thinking is one of the most critical skills a leader must have. You must view every problem from 360 degrees. You must know your own strengths and weaknesses, as well as those of your organization, your antagonists, and your supporters.'[282]

This passion for objectivity comes through time and again in the interview. Later on he reflects as follows: 'When you are in a position like mine, you can never be driven by your emotions. That doesn't mean you shouldn't get to know other people and listen to their feelings. Indeed, listening is critical for getting anything done. If you need another person to see your point of view – to come to your side in a matter such as privatisation – then you need to learn his or her motivations. But you cannot let that person's emotions sway you.'[283] Then again, he makes the simple yet profound pronouncement that 'the more responsibility you have, the more you need to be alone'.[284] A further insight into how Bernabe developed and nurtured a capacity to remain teachable in the face of criticism comes in this comment: 'I spend much of my time reading. I read reports from my staff, but I also read literature, history, and philosophy.'[285]

---

[282] Ibid.
[283] Ibid., 92.
[284] Ibid., 93.
[285] Ibid., 94.

What are some attitudinal adjustments you can make so as to be in a non-reactive position to turn criticism to your own advantage?

- *Consider that conflict goes with the territory when you are working with people:* Especially where there is creativity, there is bound to be healthy conflict. The same goes for introduction of needed change: needed or not, change is bound to generate opposition.

- *Conflict is resolvable when there is open discussion over the cause of disagreement:* Matthew 18 surely teaches us the importance of orderly and clear communication about problems in the church. Suppression of discussion of sources and causes of conflict only means failing to live in the real world where working together by nature introduces differences of opinion, etc. Sweeping tension under the carpet is neither practical nor biblical, and therefore is untenable.

- *Treat conflict as revolving around issues and not personalities:* As I have noted in my earlier book, *We Are the World: Globalisation and the Changing Face of Missions,* separating the two is not always simple. People from the two-thirds world generally have a greater problem in accepting that a frontal attack on one's position about a ministry or company issue is not an attack on the person. But, to create a working climate as a leader whereby people are freed to distinguish between these two things is going to make criticism viewed as a learning experience rather than a retreat into a nuclear war bunker shelter.

- *Conflict should involve a search for solutions for problems rather than focus on an exercise in assigning blame:* The driving motivation in team problem-solving work should be to deal with the problem through creative new solutions rather than in cleverly skewering the main culprit in the problem.

- *Conflict is a group issue:* Individual problems become the ownership of the group. Isn't that how it is supposed to be in the body of Christ: when one suffers we all suffer, when one rejoices we all rejoice? Naming and blaming is overdone in the church: we have to get over our nasty habit of shooting our wounded.[286]

An intriguing dynamic develops between leader and follower. Call it 'the law of the parrot', if you will. Some leaders over time make clear that they do not want to hear opinions, or a vision, or call the feedback what you wish, that reflects a different point of view from their own. People need to feel safe enough with their leaders to be able to speak their minds and not just rehearse and parrot back to him or her what they think the leader wants to hear from them for fear of their independence being held against them.[287] It is the soft heart of a servant leader, the leader who is teachable, that can allow for the sort of vulnerability that does not always play it safe in group think sessions. That's the sort of leadership we are advocating here.

Turning conflict to advantage because of a receptive spirit to positive lessons that can be learned from the conflict; that's what we're talking about. A singular example of this is the way certain political leaders have developed the art of winning over their enemies (as in wooing) by neutralizing them. Sometimes this altruism can lack integrity but the former US president, George Bush, strikes me as being one of those who did this in a legitimate sense, one that is consistent with what we are considering here. After winning the US presidential election of 1988 he immediately met with his defeated

---

[286] Thomas Quick, *Successful Team Building*, 67–8.
[287] Tom Marshall, *Understanding Leadership*, 23.

opponent, Michael Dukakis. He also met with his chief
rival for the nomination, Senator Robert Dole, and with
Afro-American leaders who had resisted his election,
such as Jesse Jackson and Coretta Scott King. He sought
to placate them with positions in his cabinet or reassur-
ances that they would have access to him and that he
would lend a listening ear to their concerns. For instance,
he invited Dole's wife to serve in his cabinet, as she did
ably. Some people call this 'damage control'. Perhaps this
is the sort of thing Jesus had in mind when he, by way of
commendation, called the people of this world shrewder
than the children of light (Luke 16:8,9). Nanus and
Bennis call this kind of quality necessary in leaders and
label it the Wallenda Factor, summarizing its essence
with these words: '. . . valid attacks are very useful in that
they are an opportunity to complete one's relationship
with one's own failing.'[288] They also make this astute
observation: 'Criticism is a frequent by-product of significant actions. Receptivity to criticism is as necessary as it is
loathsome.'[289]

The spirit of teachability is a humble spirit. It is
noteworthy in many women and men of God down
through church history. One thinks again of William Carey,
for example, who after 40 years in India, on his birthday,
looked back on his life and spoke of his own unworthiness,
his gratitude for God's sustaining presence amidst numerous trials, and determined to be 'more entirely devoted' to
Christ. One of his last requests was that a couplet from one
of his favourite Isaac Watt hymns be inscribed as an
epitaph on his tombstone:

---

[288] Warren Bennis and Burt Nanus, *Leaders: The Strategies for
Taking Charge*, 75.
[289] Ibid., 74.

'A wretched, poor, and helpless worm,
On Thy kind arms I fall.'[290]

What strikes me about Carey here, particularly, though, is that he was never satisfied; he never carried about the air of having arrived. There were still more worlds to conquer. He had his ear to the ground and eyes to the clouds so that he could learn still more.

The renowned Bernard of Clairvaux (1090–1153) also had this learning spirit forged on the anvil of a proper discernment of his own self. Born into a wealthy family, he entered a monastery at the age of twenty two. Among his achievements were the founding of seventy monasteries, being a pivotal figure in the healing of the papal schism of 1130, being influential in the courts of European emperors and kings, and writing voluminous mystical, theological, and devotional works. Calvin and Luther deeply appreciated his theology. Hymns attributed to him include the well-known 'Jesus The Very Thought of Thee' and 'Jesus Thou Joy of Loving Hearts'. Nevertheless, he was known as a self-effacing man who wore the cloak of power lightly. In his book, *The Steps of Humility and Pride* (1125), he stated this: 'Humility is a virtue by which a man has a low opinion of himself because he knows himself well.'[291]

Another thing that characterized all such people was their rich prayer life. They distrusted themselves sufficiently to always feel broken unless they sensed the special touch of God on their lives. That's what drove them to seek God's face. I think, for example, of the

---

[290] Timothy George, *Faithful Witness: The Life and Mission of William Carey* (Birmingham, AB: New Hope, 1991), 155, 168.
[291] Thomas Merton, *The Last of the Fathers* (New York: Harcourt, Brace and Company, 1954).

English poet and pastor John Donne, whose story of being bed-ridden by what was first feared to be the bubonic plague, then sweeping London in the 1600s, is told by Philip Yancey in *Reaching for the Invisible God*. Out of the uncertainty of why God had allowed Donne's being laid low when he had unstintingly helped those devastated by the epidemic, Donne's inability to discern God's purposes in his sickness did not drive him away from God in bitterness, but made him all the more cognizant of his full dependence on God. In his wrestling with God, like Jacob of old, Donne changed his question from 'why me' to 'how can I trust God' in this situation, even if he didn't know whether God was chastening him or if this was a natural occurrence. Out of human limitation, then, comes that growing desire to be close to God, which is partially expressed by the quality of one's prayer life.

To conclude this lengthy section, I quote thoughts along the same line from the pen of friend and fellow colleague in OM for many years, Viv Thomas: 'Our human condition puts us on the verge of disaster all the time: we continually walk a fine line between life and death, sickness and health, elation and absolute misery. The people who are in the deepest trouble are those who do not believe that this is so. If we grasp this, we are able to live lives of glorious dependency on God. We converse with him because we know we need him; it is often as raw as that. Trouble is the environment of the child.'[292]

Conclusion

Just in case you have not grasped what I have been trying to say about servant leadership in Chapter Seven,

---

[292] Viv Thomas, *Future Leader*, 27.

I close with this testimonial from the lips of the prophet Isaiah, as enshrined in Scripture in Isaiah 50:4–5. It reveals the teachability of a servant of God who had already gone through much in the way of hardships and blessings in the carrying out of his calling. Years into his ministry, he still had the attitude that he could 'learn something new every day' in order to be a vessel fitter for his Master's use.

> The Sovereign LORD has given me an instructed tongue,
> to know the word that sustains the weary.
> He wakens me morning by morning,
> wakens my ear to listen like one being taught.
> The Sovereign LORD has opened my ears,
> and I have not been rebellious;
> I have not drawn back.

8

Impartiality: Not being impressed by power

One of the iconoclastic notions of leadership nurtured in Scripture is that of giving away power instead of hoarding it. This self-giving in contrast to self-serving style of leadership, as we have repeated time and again in this book in a variety of ways, is exemplified in the Lord Jesus Christ, who did not come to be served but to serve. One of the characteristics that ties *(tys)* servanthood together across leadership styles and roles is a capacity for impartiality. In the context of leadership, impartiality is best demonstrated by a willingness to forego the privileges of power.

A startling illustration of disposable power is seen in the way the old China Inland Mission (now the Overseas Missionary Fellowship) reacted after the overthrow of the Boxer Rebellion in China in 1899–1900. The Boxers had spread throughout northern China, martyring not only national believers, but foreign missionaries. Egged on by the Empress Dowager, massacre followed massacre. By the time the Boxers had been dispersed, 188 Protestant missionaries (including some from CIM), over nineteen hundred Protestant Chinese Christians, and about thirty thousand Chinese Catholics had died for their faith. As a result, the western powers sought vengeful retribution.

Among the compensations sought was a huge indemnity of gold from the Qing government for loss of life and property.

Certain missions also sought financial compensation. However, the CIM was not among them. Their founder and leader, Hudson Taylor, said that in order to distinguish the missionaries from western imperialists, and to show to the Chinese 'the meekness and gentleness of Christ', they would not initiate claims or accept compensation from the Chinese government. What a powerful modelling of the servant leadership of Christ this was. The CIM did not take advantage of their power when they had the upper hand. They comprehended that Christian leadership and power are not to be used as leverage to get one's way; instead they perceived the importance of being oblivious to the rights and privileges of power. This I call impartiality. It is unveiled for what it is in practical ways: a penchant for identifying with followers, treating everyone as equals, submitting as missionaries to national leadership, refusing the perks of power, and identifying with the poor when contextualizing one's ministry.

Identifying with your followers

True servant leaders identify with their followers/workers/team members. They are not stand-offish. Usually you know your leader has identified with you when he or she is touched emotionally by what is happening to you, for example. We see this ever so clearly in the life of Jesus. In weeping over the grief of Mary and Martha at the death of their brother Lazarus, we see how close he had grown to them. He was one of the family. To proffer another such encounter, Christ's handling of Mary Magdalene, the promiscuous seeker, in contrast to how his host wanted to deal with her, shows how much he entered the world and experience of the common person. Sometimes leaders do not mix with their employees – except for office Christmas parties and on formal occasions. There is no entering into the lives of their people. Sometimes these sorties into the worlds of others have to be more symbolic than anything else, it is true. We talked about that earlier when the accessibility of the leader was touched on. Leaders are extremely busy people and so they cannot always preoccupy themselves with the personal problems of those working for them.

Ways that I try to demonstrate impartiality, that is, to prove that I am one of the guys ('don't treat me special') are to do things like wash or dry the dishes at church suppers, or by taking my place in the queue rather than jumping to the front, at those same suppers, as I am usually encouraged to do, or in going out of my way to joke around with the young people of the church when all the 'important' people are vying for the attention of their pastor. At my previous church, although the deacons said they would arrange for one of their number to make a special trip to the church early on Monday mornings to take the rubbish for the week out to the roadside for pick-up by the city garbage collectors, I insisted that it was just as easy for me to take care of that chore since I would be there in the building that morning anyway – which I did for five years. No big deal – but sometimes it is the little things that tip off people as to what your attitude toward them really is. As George Verwer has said, 'little things may be trivia, but they are not trivial'. Indeed, did not Jesus say that he who can be trusted in the little things will be put in charge of many things (Luke 16:10)?

One is struck by the example of so many Christian leaders in this regard, not the least of whom is George

Verwer. He has almost an irreverence with respect to the pomp and circumstance of the leader. You do not see him sitting on stage in some big Christian gathering, like the annual Keswick Convention in England or Urbana for InterVarsity Christian Fellowship students in North America, in a three piece suit. He seems thrown together with his crumpled sports jacket with either a mismatching tie or a T-shirt underneath with a picture of the world map on it, or whatever. Seeing him up close prepare for church services, or OM meetings (since he and his wife have stayed in our home several times over the years), my sense is not that he deliberately thumbs his nose at the evangelical establishment (although he might have done so when he first started out) but that he is just indifferent to such matters. He is a truly impartial person in his leadership, identifying as easily and as much with the everyday pew warmer as he does with the rich and famous.

From another century one thinks of Charles Spurgeon for example. Although he pastored a church of thousands for 40 years and spawned innumerable ministries which demanded his attention, Spurgeon made time for the average parishioner. He either visited 70 people from his church every week on Saturday and Tuesday afternoons or he received enquirers at the church. He believed strongly in personal evangelism, always making time to share the gospel on a one to one basis, even though he saw thousands converted by his pulpit ministry. In this down-to-earth approach with his people, Spurgeon exhibited this quality of impartiality that I am talking about here.

I guess impartiality is another way of saying that people are treated as equals by the leader. Leighton Ford has picked up on this essential quality in the leader when he observes that 'great leaders have a passion for equality. History defines examples, such as Alexander

the Great, sharing his food with his men, calling them by
their first names, marching along with them in the heat,
and being the first over the wall in battle'.[293] Mahatma
Gandhi also comes to mind in this respect. Why was he
loved by the untouchable and across all caste lines in
India? Perhaps because he dressed in homespun kadi
(spun by himself incidentally), married inter-caste, and
consistently showed his disregard for entrenched Hindu
elitism. He was an impartial leader because he treated
everyone as his equal.

What a challenge this is for the leader in any era. The
Bible is crystal-clear about the paramount ethical importance of equality in the body of Christ. There can be no
partiality on the basis of race, gender, or economic status
in the church (Gal. 3:28), for to act in worldly patterns of
discrimination is to skew the world's perception of who
God is, the impartial one (Acts 10:34,35).[294] Inclusivism is
not just a politically correct concept but a biblical one
(Eph. 2:11–21). The Bible comes down hard on church
folk who use wealth as a basis to marginalize those less
well off in the congregation (James 2:1–7). When we see a
pastor or Christian leader becoming the focus of attention and the locus of power, inevitably they are doing so
by climbing over the backs of those they are meant to
serve, in order to get to the top. Such politicizing of
leadership is what Richard Foster has in mind when he
says, 'Those who take on the mantle of leadership do so
for the sake of others, not for their own sake. Their

---

[293] Leighton Ford, *Transforming Leadership*, 209.
[294] For a full biblical word study of *impartiality* and of the issue
of equality in the church see my book, *We Are the World:
Globalisation and the Changing Face of Missions*, especially
pp. 9–15.

concern is to meet the needs of people, not to advance their own reputations.'[295]

Kenon Callaghan fascinatingly documents the trend in western society that has resulted in clergymen being removed from a pedestal of adoration and respect to that of ordinariness. He claims that in an effort to be put back on the pedestal the pastor has sought to gain recognition and honour through professionalism.[296] Through increasing emphasis on education the pastor has been put into the same class as the professional, that is, as with doctors or lawyers. In fact, ours is the best educated generation of pastors the church has yet seen. It is not at all unusual for a pastor to have his or her doctorate whereas a generation ago it would have been a rarity; such theologians would only have been found in seminaries. Not so now. But has this focus on professionalism made us more spiritual? Decidedly not!

One might also make the argument that the establishment of the office of 'bishop' in the early church may very well have arisen out of power-grabbing as much as it did out of a confusion as to what Scripture was really saying on the subject. After all, the words for 'elders' and 'bishops', one must admit, are used somewhat loosely and interchangeably in the NT (e.g., cf. Acts 20:17 with v. 28; cf. 1 Peter 5:1,2; 1 Tim. 5:17–19). The case has been well made by various theologians that the NT stress is not on holding offices in local churches but on exercising of spiritual gifts.[297] The way that church office-holders have been given special perks of power did not really strike me as being an issue until I first went to India. There it was that

---

[295] Richard Foster, *The Challenge of the Disciplined Life* (San Francisco: HarperCollins, 1998), 235.

[296] Kenon Callaghan, *Effective Church Leadership*, 6–8.

[297] An example of this argument well-defended is in Michael Green, *Freed To Serve*, especially Chapter Five.

I saw for the first time what I have subsequently discovered to be very much a reality in some denominations of the west too, church leaders living in luxury. Indian Protestant bishops live in large compounds in well-off circumstances, surrounded by poverty. Symbolizing their privileges of power – apart from their spacious and secluded compounds – are their chauffeur-driven cars, waiting at their beck and call 24 hours a day. No wonder the on-looking Hindu erroneously assumes that Christianity is a western religion. Of course the servant sweeping the driveway lined by magnificent potted plants assumes that it is a religion of the rich . . . which came via the white-skinned missionaries from America or England, who similarly, or so their parents told them, lived in compounds where their opulence (in relation to the masses) marked them out as being the equivalents of the Brahmin caste.

Refusing the perks of power

Refusing the perks of power is both a conscious and an unconscious thing. But it relates very much to impartiality and therefore to servanthood. Intentionally Jesus thumbed his nose at the religious establishment by mixing with the publicans and prostitutes: he came to call not the righteous but sinners to repentance. Little ways we can identify with the average member of the public by not accepting the special privileges that come with evangelical recognition include things like not allowing our church board to assign us the parking spot closest to the front door of the church with a nice parking sign attached (speaking to pastors here). Please do not tell me, pastor, sir, that you want to be a good steward of your time and so do not want to waste time walking from the far end of the parking lot! (It wouldn't hurt for a few pastors to find any means of losing weight!) Some extra benefits are actually essential working tools – like the pastor's allowance for books, which most churches provide. But do we really need to be referred to as 'reverend'? Should we pastors be any more called to the ministry than the woman who is a Sunday School teacher and a pharmacist? Why do we not give her a special title? I respect the former pastor of Guildford Baptist Church in England and Bramalea Baptist Church in Toronto, Justin Dennison, who insists that his flock not call him 'pastor' or 'reverend'. He is trying in a small way to signal to his people that the church is made up of the priesthood of all believers. He has refused a perk of power.

Or what about the missionary who still insists on living in a missionary compound, isolated from all the grime, disease, and lower class people on its periphery? I say banish missionary compounds. They are a relic of the colonial age. Live with the people you reach. So what if you get malaria or typhoid? Such is the cost of doing business. Instead many of the national churches of the historical missionary fields of the modern missionary movement to this day still treat the white man with the deference that is a contradiction of the levelling effect of the gospel (Eph. 6:9). Mother Teresa made a profound impact on Indian society in part because of her unconventional commitment to impartiality.

Then there are the big areas. This has a lot to do with advancement through the ranks of pastoral ministry, academic institutions, and parachurch organizational life. Grasping after bigger churches and grander salaries has as much to do with the average turnover of pastors in churches every 4.5 years as it does with churches or pastors facing conflict that gets resolved only by the pastor moving on. What most churches need – or so the experts tell us – is pastors who will stay for 15 years or more. Churches grow best with stability (and good leadership of course!); it takes years for churches and their pastors to get used to each other and then form the synergy which will make the best of their combined assets. Martin Luther was no fool when he stated, 'there are three conversions necessary: the conversion of the heart, the mind, and the purse.'[298] Indicting the dark side of this upward mobility among Christian workers, Cheryl Forbes says this:

> As difficult as it might be to do, Christians must say no to power, individually and corporately. A decision for power is antithetical to a desire for God. We must reject the reasoning that says without power we cannot achieve; without power we cannot work. Power may help for a while, but ultimately it will side-track, discourage, and neutralise us. Rather than working, we spend our time and energy trying to protect our power. And this, if we understand the true nature of work, is unacceptable.[299]

We must reject the notion that influence in kingdom-building and importance in God's scheme of things has anything to do with the number of people we preach to on Sunday, the number of converts we make, or the size of our budget. According to Jesus, the first will be last and the last first in the kingdom of God: heaven will be full of surprises. In not being impressed by size when it comes to ministry, and by people's status in society when we relate to them, we are demonstrating the even-handedness

---

[298] Quoted in Richard Foster, *The Challenge of the Disciplined Life*, 20.
[299] Cheryl Forbes, *The Religion of Power*, 146.

that is a function of servanthood.

Again, church history is replete with examples of those who learned to say 'small is beautiful'. One of the outstanding figures in this regard is Chrysostom (AD 349–407), a dominant preacher of his time. As bishop of Constantinople at a time when Constantine had legitimized Christianity in the Roman Empire and thus gave its champions access to considerable power and perks, the golden-mouthed preacher, as Chrysostom was called, insisted on identifying with the average member of his congregation. He refused to give the lavish parties the bishops were used to mounting. He would not ride around in a chariot as important people like him were wont to do, and he was not a frequent visitor at the imperial palace. In the first year of his being bishop, he saved enough money to build a hospital. His activity among the poor was renowned. Yes, Chrysostom understood the principle of impartiality.

Another bishop, the famous theologian, Augustine of Hippo (AD 354–430), did not live in splendour like many bishops but insisted that his priests live with him in a monastic establishment in the bishop's house. They together then took a vow of poverty and celibacy. His sermons contained many exhortations to the rich to give to the poor. He muttered these words: 'I do not intend to spend a puffed-up existence in ecclesiastical positions: my thoughts are on the day when I must render my account for the sheep committed to me by the Prince of Shepherds.'[300]

Finally we single out an Englishman. John Wesley practised what he preached when it came to living frugally – this in spite of the fact that the royalties from his multitude of published writings (£1,400 annually)

---

[300] Quoted in Peter Brown, *Augustine of Hippo* (Berkeley, CA: University of California Press, 1967), 208.

made him one of England's richest people in his day and age. Instead of letting his expenses rise with his income – like I confess I tend to do – he kept his expenses to the £28 he spent in 1731 when he first began to carefully follow what he felt were biblical principles of stewardship.[301] He believed in earning all you can, saving all you can, and giving away all you can! In 1744, Wesley wrote, 'When I die if I leave behind me ten pounds . . . you and mankind can bear witness against me, that I have lived and died a thief and a robber.'[302] Indeed, when he passed away in 1791 the only money mentioned in his will and found were the few coins retrieved from his pockets and dresser drawers.

Identifying with the poor

Let us go one step further. In our determination to intentionalize impartiality, to celebrate the *oikomene* (one people) of the body of Christ and the world (Acts 17:26), we need to also remember that the gospel is for the poor, citing the words of Jesus himself: 'The Spirit of the Lord is on me, because he has anointed me to preach good news to the poor. He has sent me to proclaim freedom for the prisoners and recovery of sight for the blind, to release the oppressed, to proclaim the year of the Lord's favour' (Luke 4:18,19). This impartiality in terms of deliberately identifying with the poor cuts both ways. It is not good enough for those in the church to tell missionaries that contextualization requires them, as

---

[301] Charles E. White, 'What Wesley Practiced and Preached About Money', *Mission Frontiers Bulletin* (September/October 1994), 23.
[302] Ibid., 24.

they labour in the two-thirds world, especially, to seek out the poor. Our urban churches in the western world need to face the fact that they have too frequently abandoned the inner city and headed for the suburbs for a comfortable, sanitized middle class lifestyle undisturbed by the homeless, the unemployed, and the helpless new immigrant.

I find it fascinating, as I presently pastor a Chinese church, to discover that Chinatown in downtown Toronto has experienced a demographic shift in the last decade or so. The first wave of Chinese immigrants populating the Spadina-Dundas area of the city came from Hong Kong and Singapore – essentially from the Cantonese speaking areas of south-east Asia. Subsequently the principal wave of immigrants of the nineties and into the new millennium have been from mainland China, Mandarin-speaking Chinese for the most part. The former were often wealthy and the latter generally poor. As the downtown has been encroached on by the Mandarin-speaking immigrants, the Cantonese have shifted to midtown and uptown. In the process, the demographics of the downtown Chinese churches have changed. The Cantonese are increasingly abandoning the downtown, leaving Mandarin-speaking churches full of seekers and new converts without the depth of leadership and financial resources to prosper (although this is a generalization).

Lest Caucasians get too comfortable, we have done the same thing. Large inner city churches, like Knox Presbyterian in Toronto, adjacent to the University of Toronto, are filled with commuters (to church) and students. Large segments of congregations like Knox are uninvolved with the community surrounding the church. Knox, for instance, is within a block radius of the most infamous abortion clinic in the city and a host of nationalities residing on the side streets.[303] No longer do such churches represent a cross section of the neighbourhoods they are found in and so are ineffective in evangelizing in their own communities. A loss of will to rub shoulders with the disfranchised of society is surely a reflection of an abandonment of true servanthood. Genuine impartiality is missing all too often in such contexts.

Missiologist Jonathan Ingleby is even more adamant about the failure of the church in contextualizing by saying that most local contexts actually have more than one aspect to them, and that usually the more powerful group(s) within the local context are catered to – in the name of 'contextualization' of course.[304] He claims that when the church sides with the status quo in a community that almost always means siding with the dominant of several cultures or interest groups in that community. Whenever a serious attempt is made to work with those who are marginalized in society, he argues, it arouses the opposition of the powerful in that society. However, he claims, the gospel is not neutral, tilting mission toward the poor.

John Stott is even more withering in his jaundiced view of the church and its leaders vis-à-vis the posturing of impartiality that is associated with servanthood.

---

[303] To Knox's credit, it does have a history of reaching out into the surrounding community. Our church (Chinese Gospel Church) opens its doors Thursday evenings during the winter months for the homeless of Toronto to have a place to sleep in and to be fed overnight. This programme is called Out Of The Cold and different churches across the city open their doors different nights of the week to make this ministry possible.

[304] Jonathan Ingleby, 'Trickling Down or Shaking the Foundations: Is Contextualization Neutral?', *Missiology: An International Review*, Vol. 25 (2), April 1997, 183–7.

Throughout its long and variegated career ... the Church has seldom cultivated a humble, sensitive attitude of listening to God's Word. Instead, it has frequently done what it has been forbidden to do, namely become conformist. It has accommodated itself to the prevailing culture, leaped on board all the trendiest bandwagons, and hummed all the popular tunes. Whenever the church does this, it reads Scripture through the world's eyes, and rationalises its own unfaithfulness ...

It is too easy to criticize our Christian forebears for their blindness. It is much harder to discover our own. What will posterity see as the chief Christian blind spot of the twentieth century? I do not know. But I suspect it will have something to do with the economic oppression of the Third World and the readiness with which western Christians tolerate it, and acquiesce it.[305]

If it is true, as John Stott among others claims,[306] that most poverty is the fault of society rather than of the poor themselves (the Bible's emphasis too), Christian leaders must set the pace in personally modelling sacrificial giving and involvement with the poor, as well as seeking to influence systemic political change so as to rectify some of the problems. I would therefore agree with Stott's radical call.

The Old Testament economy which promised wealth also commanded the care of the poor. And the rich man in the parable of Jesus found himself in hell not because of his wealth but because of his neglect of the beggar at his gate. That is, Dives indulged himself at the very time Lazarus was starving.

---

[305] John Stott, 'The Authority and Relevance of the Bible in the Modern World,' *Crux*, June 1980, 17.
[306] John Stott, *Issues Facing Christians Today* (Bombay: Gospel Literature Service, 1989), 222.

In the light of these . . . biblical truths, and of the contemporary destitution of millions, it is not possible for affluent Christians to 'stay rich' in the sense of accepting no modification of economic lifestyle. We cannot maintain a 'good life' (of extravagance) and a 'good conscience' simultaneously.[307]

Leaders must show the way. This will require the sacrificial love that perceives impartiality as being essential to the practice of servant leadership. Similarly, the missionary community must be prepared to live more sacrificially in order to identify with the very people it is reaching. It is not enough to claim (although admittedly true) that already considerable counting of the cost of following Christ has been engaged in, in order to move out cross-culturally.[308] Only those filled with the servant heart of Father God will take it a step further.

One final test of impartiality. Who do you defend when the person being maligned is not present? A good test of impartiality is loyalty to the reputation of the powerless, not just the ones whose favour you want to be sure to curry. Covey puts it this way: 'One of the most important ways to manifest integrity is to be loyal to those who are not present. In so doing, we build the trust of those who are present. When you defend those who are absent, you retain the trust of those present . . . It's how you treat the one that reveals how you treat the ninety-nine, because everyone is ultimately a one.'[309]

---

[307] Ibid., 226.

[308] Jonathan J. Bonk convincingly demonstrates how the modern missionary movement has sent missionaries as affluent propagators of the gospel and of how this must change, in his book *Missions and Money: Affluence as a Western Missionary Problem* (Maryknoll, NY: Orbis Books, 1991).

[309] Stephen Covey, *7 Habits of Highly Effective People*, 196–7.

Submitting to national leadership

With the emergence of an exploding church in the two-thirds world, which now outstrips the western world church proportionately by a ratio of 4:1, the western world church, when it comes to missions, cannot act as if it belongs in the driver's seat any more.[310] It is now estimated that there are one hundred and sixty thousand missionaries from the two-thirds world – for the first time since the first centuries of church history outnumbering western world missionaries.[311] Missions cannot be construed as the west's burden any more: nor should it be since the great commission is addressed to the whole church, instructing the whole church to reach the whole world with the whole gospel for Christ. With that misconception gone (or at least assuming only its proportional share of responsibility) should come a realigning of the locus of power to the emerging churches and their mission agencies. It is the day when the meaning of 'equal partnership' can take on added significance.

This insistence on indigenization holds true whether we are talking about de-westernizing international mission agencies or on-site western missionaries working in church planting in their maturing stages. In this regard, Paul Hiebert makes astute observations with these words:

> We must also allow local leaders the greatest privilege we allow ourselves, namely, the right to make mistakes and learn from them.

---

[310] Patrick Johnstone, *Operation World* 5th ed. (Grand Rapids, MI: Zondervan, 1993), 25.

[311] Larry Keyes and Larry Pate, 'Two-Thirds World Missions: The Next One Hundred Years', *Missiology: An International Review* 21(2) (April 1993), 187–206.

The three 'self' principles continue to guide much of contemporary mission planning. They make an important point – that young churches are equal and independent members in the worldwide community of churches. Today, however, many are arguing that we must move beyond autonomy to partnership. In the name of self-support, mission agencies too often withhold funds that would help young churches carry on effective evangelism. Our goal is not to establish isolated churches that work alone, but to sustain churches that share a unity of fellowship and a common mission to the world.[312]

Another way missionaries – and their missions – can shed their ethnocentrism, like a butterfly its cocoon, leaving behind impartiality, is to ensure that their denominational or parachurch mission structures are de-westernized. I identify this in my earlier writings, as in this observation:

Today Westerners serving Christ cross-culturally may not be guilty of trying to convert 'natives' to Anglo-American culture. After all, the tools of anthropology and the other social sciences have dealt with the ignorance of our previous generations of missionaries! Let us not be guilty though of insisting that the national missionaries be converted to our way of doing missions. That would be just one more way we demonstrate we have been blinded by the spirit of pride which is at the heart of ethnocentrism [racial prejudice]![313]

[312] Paul G. Hiebert, *Anthropological Insights for Missionaries* (Grand Rapids, MI: Baker Book House, 1994), 194.
[313] J. David Lundy, 'Moving Beyond Internationalizing the Mission Force', *International Journal of Frontier Missions* 16(3) (Fall 1999), 155.

What are some of those predominantly western world ways of doing things in missions? A tendency toward excessive individualism. A lack of respect for our leaders with an overemphasis on the democratization of the decision-making processes. A rigid and selective way of interpreting the biblical data concerning the resolving of interpersonal conflict. A subtle deference given to the eloquent and outspoken in public forums at the expense of the good listener. Confrontational handling of issues and policy decisions instead of brokering of consensus behind the scenes. A tendency to think only linearly. An obsession with time management at the expense of relationship development.[314] The bottom line is that impartiality means being (or becoming) blind to the assumption that our way of doing things is the best way! It means keeping an open mind and teachable spirit in relation to the disparate sides of the church globally as together we partner in penetrating the final frontiers with the gospel.

Different but equal

There is no profundity in venturing to say that the Bible in teaching the priesthood of all believers (1 Peter 2:5) is preventing us in the church from putting our spiritual leaders in an elitist category of their own. Distinctions made on the basis of the gifts of the Spirit, then, are only to underline the varieties of service needed to make the church function up to its full potential. Thus Ephesians 4, after listing a sampling of spiritual gifts (v. 11) then goes on to illustrate through a vivid metaphor how the church

---

[314] These cultural dissimilarities between east and west (or north and south) and how they impact international missions are dealt with at some length in David Lundy, *We Are the World*.

matures, ending with the telling phrase, 'as each part does its work' (v. 16). In other words, there is no building itself up in love if each person is not using his or her own gift(s). Impartiality. That is what the dynamic of body life teaches us (1 Cor. 12:21–25). The pastor or Christian leader who postures that is a servant leader.

In practice, this impartiality through acknowledging and celebrating of equality may take different forms. It might mean allowing a team (of which the pastor is a part) planning out the whole order of corporate worship services (as our church does), and by not making the pastor the dominant force in the outworking of ministry in the services by involving many people (although the pastor may still do most of the preaching). It may mean not arbitrarily (even though possessing the authority on paper) superimposing responsibilities or programmes on people who have had no part in the decision-making process.[315] At root is the understanding that being a leader may make you different from the rest of the group but that does not change the fact that everyone is equal in God's sight in the group (Rom. 2:11). In turn, that self and group understanding of fundamental equality frees the leader to equip people for the work of the ministry rather than feeling that the leader has to do all the ministry him or herself (Eph. 4:12).

Conclusion

Impartiality. More easily said than done! How do you really know when you have achieved this standard of servanthood? The founder of the Navigators, Lorne

---

[315] Rex D. Edwards, 'Service Over Self-Interest', *Ministry* (November 1997), 19.

Sanny, gave an answer to the test of servant leadership in this way. 'How do you know when you have a servant attitude? By how you react when you are treated like one.'[316] We have been addressing that spirit of humility in different ways in this chapter. It reveals a face which is pock-marked by impartiality: through refusing to take undue advantage of the perks of power, by not allowing oneself to be put in the limelight any more than necessary, by deliberately associating with the lowly, and by identifying with your followers. Or, to put it in the words of another Navigator: 'Christian leadership, therefore, is not *exclusive* but *inclusive*. Its fundamental nature is not *elitist*, but *exemplary*. Christian leaders primarily are not a special group, exclusive and elitist; they are an integral part of the whole, and they serve as examples to the whole.'[317]

---

[316] Kenneth O. Gangel, *Feeding and Leading*, 56.
[317] Doug Sparks, 'Going Beyond Good Management', *Discipleship Journal* (January 1982), 6.

9

Identifiability: Being sensitive to the cultural context

Should it be only missionaries who are contextual experts? Of course not. At least you cannot convince secular companies that they need to disregard their markets, their customers. Procter & Gamble, maker of fabled products like Ivory Soap, studies its customers painstakingly so as to deliver products they will buy. Every year it therefore conducts 1.5 million telephone calls surveying its customers and potential customers. Warren Bennis, management guru, calls this 'mastering the context'. Hershey and Blanchard label it 'situational leadership'. As a matter of fact, that's been one of the 'big ideas' of this book: suiting one's style of leadership according to the context one is working in, whether that context be defined by the people you work with or the audience you are trying to reach with your message or product. Understanding the importance of identifying with the context of one's leadership explains in part why increasingly executives of secular companies are spending their time outside their organizations. They are developing alliances and cultivating relationships, that is, trying to understand the external environment to which their company must relate.[318] And in a world of

---

[318] Rosabeth Moss Kanter, *The Change Masters*, 5

breath-taking, speed-of-light change, you cannot assume that just because 'that's the way we've always done it' has worked before, such tradition will keep you growing and profitable!

The receptor culture

Since the gospel is distinct from human culture and yet is expressed in cultural contexts and develops cultural accretions, servant leaders cannot operate in a vacuum either. We learned this as missionaries, as we absorbed the tools of social sciences newly-emerging since the Second World War, and then reread our Bibles to see that the context is relevant to the communication of the unchanging message. Missionaries must learn not only the language of the people they are trying to reach for Christ cross-culturally, that culture being what missiologists call the *receptor culture*, but the culture's customs, symbols, rituals – in a word, its worldview.

But all great church leaders have similarly absorbed the importance of identifying with the people they are trying to reach, whether that be Paul at Ephesus, relating to both Jews and Gentiles, or Rick Warren of the Saddleback Valley Community Church in Orange County, California in the new millennium.[319]

The leader who ignores the environment he or she works in does so at his or her own peril. A case in point is the demise of a nationwide department store chain, Eaton's,

---

[319] Rick Warren for instance has a brilliant chapter in *The Purpose Driven Church* in which he identifies the stereotypical person his church is targeting to reach for Christ, whom they call 'Saddleback Sam' (see pages 155–172 in the book). Their whole progamme revolves around drawing in this sort of unbelieving person.

Canada's equivalent to the Marks & Spencer chain of stores in Great Britain. After 130 years in existence in the year 2000, Eaton's, on the verge of bankruptcy, liquidated its stock, closed its scores of stores across the country, and sold its assets to a rival company. A cultural icon, Eaton's was thought by the general populace to be impregnable. It earned its competitive success by stressing customer service and dependable quality merchandise. As late as the 1930s, Eaton's captured 60 per cent of the Canadian department store market. However, by 1997, that edge had disappeared and it held only ten per cent of the trade. The big reason for the demise of the venerable company is that it lost touch with its customers, failing to adjust to the changing culture in Canadian society as a whole.

What a lesson for the church and its leaders. We must understand our cultural context or die. That can be a complex task. Most people do not just live in a mono-chrome culture. As hard as exegeting your culture might be, the servant leader knows that understanding those he or she is reaching or leading is the key to winning their hearts. Viv Thomas puts it this way: 'The reason why leadership is often so complex is that good leaders inevitably face many directions at once. There is a continual conversation between the people of God and the huge context within which they seek to live out their lives. Great leadership encounters the conversation and complexity and does not seek to simplify that which defies simplicity.'[320] Effective international leaders assume difference until similarity is proven. This attitude and approach keeps such leaders open-minded, inquisitive, and empathetic in relating to people of other cultures. Leith Anderson, pastor of a large and growing church in the American

---

[320] Viv Thomas, *Future Leader*, 130.

mid-west, says much the same thing in relating cultural
sensitivity to pastoring in the local context: 'If leaders allow
themselves to become isolated in the problems and perspectives of leadership, they lose touch with those whom
they claim to lead. This is a subtle thing that can easily
happen. When they lose contact with people and society,
they no longer understand and become ineffective . . . The
leader who leads must understand the culture, which
comes from reading, listening, visiting, and observing.'[321]
New millennium church leaders need to refocus, away
from their church committees and running of churches
internally, to immersing themselves in the worlds of their
parishioners and their neighbourhoods. Callaghan elo-
quently says much the same thing in exhorting as follows:

> In our time, a new understanding of the nature of
> leadership needs to be grown forward. We need a
> foundational understanding that the focus of leadership
> will be *in the world*, not in the church.
>
> We need an understanding of the nature of leadership
> that is more proactive and less reactive. We need an
> understanding of leadership that is more intentional and
> less passive, more relational and less organizational, more
> missional and less institutional.
>
> The day of the churched culture [in the western world] is
> over. The day of the mission field has come.[322]

The organizational culture

Both missionaries and Christian leaders of all stripes
make a fatal mistake in thinking that they only have to

---

[321] Leith Anderson, *Dying for Change*, 190.
[322] Kenon Callaghan, *Effective Church Leadership*, 21.

learn the culture of the receptor group. Unless they are functioning in ministry on their own, they also have to learn an organizational culture. That is the culture of the organization or ministry for which they work. The Chinese-Canadian church I am pastoring in the heart of Toronto has an English-speaking congregation which is neither fully Canadian (culturally, even though a high percentage of its people have been born in Canada or otherwise are Canadian citizens) nor fully Chinese (they – perjoratively in my opinion – call themselves *bananas*: 'yellow on the outside and white on the inside'). In order for me to minister effectively in their midst I must master the bi-cultural nature of this unique subculture. However, many pastors do not establish themselves effectively in their churches, not because of their own or their congregation's spiritual problems, but because they have not mastered the organi zational culture. They have been so intent on winning people for Christ that they have been like bulls in china shops among the people already saved – the ones who pay their salaries, decide the future direction of the church, etc.

When my wife and I shifted some years ago from serving as missionaries with Operation Mobilisation to serving with Arab World Ministries, we had a steep learning curve. AWM was one hundred years old. It had a much more Anglo-American influence than the globalized OM. OM was younger and AWM was peppered with sea-soned veterans labouring in a tough mission field. While OM was free-wheeling and more open to change, AWM moved cautiously. For instance, it had a Mission Manual inches thick, governing everything from how to relate to the ecumenical movement to what sort of hospitality rate to give when visiting another missionary overnight. To insist that I serve the same way in AWM as I had for the six previous years I had served with OM would have been to cut off my nose to spite my face. Not always smoothly accomplished, nevertheless, I assure you that I made a point of learning the organizational culture of AWM.

Each church or ministry, then, has a unique culture that must be respected by its leadership in order to flourish. Addressing pastors about this, James Dobson Ministries' pastor to pastors, London, lovingly say this: 'Like a family likeness, every congregation bears a likeness to all other churches. But each church has more distinctives than similarities ... Consequently using a church's uniqueness is a magnificently important factor in developing a flourishing ministry in any congregation. God gives uniqueness to a church for us to recognize and to use. Your church, like every snowflake and raindrop, has been created quite unlike any other.'[323]

Only when it comes to starting from scratch can a pastor/church planter afford the luxury of ignoring the inner customs and traditions and philosophy of ministry that power all churches. But then again, you still have to exegete the culture of the people with whom you expect to fill your fledgling church. Wisely Rick Warren comments about this need for contextualization when learning from the churches that have grown well: 'I encourage [churches] to filter what they've learned from us through their context and personality. God has a custom ministry for each church. Your church has a unique thumbprint that God has given it. But you can learn from models without becoming a clone!'[324] Later on he humorously says the following along the same lines:

> Churches that expect the unchurched to show up simply because they build a building and hang out a 'We're Open'

---

[323] H.B. London and Neil Wiseman, *The Heart of a Great Pastor*, 20–1.

[324] Rick Warren, *The Purpose Driven Church*, 68.

sign are deluding themselves. People don't voluntarily jump into your boat. You must penetrate their culture.

To penetrate any culture you must be willing to make small concessions in matters of style in order to gain a hearing. For example, our church has adopted the casual, informal style and dress of the southern California community we minister in.[325]

The incarnation and the principle of identification

The meaning of Christ's incarnation has deepened for me as a result of living in India. There the Hinduism that is most popular is the *bhakti* movement. *Bhakti* means *devotion* and refers to how Hindus are able to love their gods. The deities the common Hindu identifies with the most are the *avatars*, that is, the ones who have allegedly taken on human form, like Ram and Krishna. There are contrasts between Hindu avatars and the God-man Jesus Christ, however. In the avatars there is the emergence of Vishnu onto the human stage, but not of the ultimate God or *Paramatma*. Christ, on the other hand, was fully ultimate God in descending to earth (John 1:1,14). He carried the divine imprint on himself when he walked this earth (Heb. 1:3). Furthermore, in a sense there is this understanding that the avatars did not fully enter human experience. They delivered people from evil but were not affected by it in the same way that Christ was tempted in every way as we are, being fully human, yet without sin (Heb. 4:15).[326]

The *passibility* of God is an important theological concept. It refers to the capacity and reality of God

[325] Ibid., 196.
[326] P.T. Chandapilla, *The Master Trainer*, 1–4.

suffering because he is affected emotionally by our world, by how we love or rebel against him. It claims that he is able to experience feelings but without their fallen aspects; references in Scripture to God having feelings, then, are not always to be interpreted as anthropomorphic. That being said, it must not go unremarked that the classic notion of this aspect of God's attributes is quite the opposite, that is, that God is *impassible*.[327] The basic argument goes like this: were God to change, that implies that it is a move toward perfection or away from perfection. Of late, in particular, the suggestion has been made that this idea about God's nature was borrowed uncritically from Greek thought by the early church. According to Philo, for example, where Scripture implies the suffering of God, it is using a metaphor which should not be taken literally with reference to the divine essence – although humans may experience God as suffering, or compassionate, or whatever.[328]

However, we counter with arguing that God's passibility is no more pristinely expressed than in the incarnation. Christ's suffering, especially on the cross, was real. 1 Peter in particular seeks to establish this dimension of Christ's earthly existence (e.g. 1 Peter 2:22–24). And it is through the example of this incarnation that we as followers of Christ are to similarly be incarnational in our ministry (1 John 2:6). Surely that is the thrust of Philippians 2 as it links Christ's incarnation to the way we are to relate to each other on the horizontal level: 'Your attitude [in relation to each other] should be the same as that of Christ Jesus' (v. 5).

---

[327] A good survey of this theological question is found in Alister McGrath, *Christian Theology: An Introduction* (Oxford: Blackwell Publishers, 1994), 213–9.

[328] Cited in ibid., 214–5.

When it comes to leadership, then, identifiability is crucial to expressing servant leadership. It models the kind of leadership Jesus offered by virtue of his incarnation. Chandapilla summarizes this connection well when he states:

> The incarnation is the greatest, noblest and most ultimate event in the interaction between and integration of the 'spiritual-divine' and the 'physical-human'. . . These are the reasons why the incarnation becomes unique and central to the Christian faith. This is central also to the whole concept of leadership training . . .
>
> It may be stated as a principle, then, that as a first step in leadership training the trainer must build the bridge himself, cross the barrier and come to the level of the trainee. The lofty and inaccessible ideas or experiences must be brought to the level and reach of the low. This is incarnation in application and it is always the responsibility of the Master or trainer to incarnate himself.[329]

It is my prediction that at the heart of pastoral leadership in the twenty-first century in the western world, will be a rediscovery of what some are now calling the 'missional church' model. As the world has come to our doorstep, we are having to rethink *mission*. We are learning that we have to re-evangelize 'Christian lands', whether that be Great Britain, Germany, the USA, or Canada. This will lead to a re-examination of the theology of the church. Churches, functioning now as they are in an adversarial, post-Christian context, can no longer possess the luxury of choosing between *edification of the saints* or *evangelization of the lost* as their main calling. The two will fittingly and biblically be integrated so that all church programmes

---

[329] P.T. Chandapilla, *The Master Trainer*, 4.

and ministries will be carried out with a culture-of-witness mindset. That is to say, seeker driven or seeker sensitive churches will not be well-integrated enough to justify their outreach thrusts. Those emphases are too one-sided. Rather than creating programmes that virtually only have the lost in mind – whether that be the main worship service or the small cell groups – we will instinctively be inclusive, that is, allowing non-believers to 'sit in on' what we do as church. Friendship evangelism will be a part of that new thrust but it will represent more than that. Missional churches will see that 'making disciples' is on a continuum. Our goal will not just be to make converts, but to see conversion as part of the process of making disciples, which is the real mission (Matt. 28:18–20). Thus we will nurture them all along the path toward presenting 'everyone perfect in Christ' (Col. 1:28). Therefore, they will see how we love God as we worship him together Sunday mornings; they will sit in on our discipleship classes for new believers as they seek for ultimate truth; they will find warm community in the need-meeting small groups for believers even though they are really on the outside of the family looking in. Believers, then, must be allowed and taught to feel at home around non-Christians and this will require a volte-face with regard to the concept of separation from the world. But it will also breathe new life into old wineskins and we will move seamlessly back and forth between seeking the lost and serving the saved. It is an incarnational and an identificational model of church.

Surely this is the kind of thing that missiologist Van Engel must have in mind when he urges,

> The Church is uniquely the body of Jesus Christ who is uniquely the God-man, at once divine and human, other-worldly and this-worldly. It is not by accident but by design

that the Church which is his body should be 'in the world, but not of the world'; should be at once a fallen, human institution, and a perfect, divine organism. Only as we join the human and divine aspects of the Church's nature in a unified perspective can we possibly arrive at a true understanding of the Church's mission.[330]

Double contextualization

What we are really talking about here is the ability of leaders – whether they are elders, pastors, mission executives, or missionaries – to engage the culture and the text critically. It is a kind of double contextualization. Leaders need to be people of the word, able to accurately handle the word of truth, because they have wrestled with the biblical texts in their historical and cultural contexts as written thousands of years ago, so that they know what God was saying to those people then. Finally leaders have to be students of their own culture (or the culture they work in) so as to then make that eternal Word relevant to today and the immediate cultural context.[331] Identification then must cut two ways: understanding the word as originally given, and then applying it fittingly to the contemporary situation the leader is immersed in.

Much emphasis has been given in our seminaries and Bible colleges historically to comprehending the world of Jesus' day, of Bible times, but not as much, unfortunately, to grasping the culture in which one serves as a leader

---

[330] Charles Van Engel, *God's Missionary People: Rethinking the Purpose of the Local Church* (Grand Rapids, MI: Baker Book House, 1995), 44.

[331] Paul Hiebert, *Anthropological Insights for Missionaries*, 202–3, 218–19.

today. Consequently, too often our higher learning institutions have produced non-identifying leaders who lead churches as if they were stuck in a time warp of the Reformation era, or of mission field ministries still in a colonial framework. It cannot be stressed enough the importance of the servant leader spending time with his or her people and in the community. This approach to leading presupposes more of a shepherding as opposed to a CEO model. It is modelled supremely in the Lord Jesus Christ, the good shepherd (John 10) but has a long-established history in the OT where Yahweh is Israel's shepherd (Psalm 23) and the Messiah is to come in a line of shepherds (Jer. 3:15). The NT word *poimon* is found 18 times and describes the one who protects his sheep (Acts 20:28), the one who leads his sheep (1 Cor. 9:7), and the one who lays down his life for his sheep (1 Peter 5:1–3). In fact, the word *pastor* comes from the Latin word for shepherd.

To shepherd one's people, then, connotes the idea of intimately being acquainted with one's people, which in turn implies spending time with them. We have talked about that in previous chapters in terms of the leader being accessible, approachable, vulnerable, and of being available to mentor, disciple, and model the Christian life. Counselling has not been reflected on too much herein. Nevertheless it is an essential element in leadership and will be engaged in whole-heartedly by the leader possessing a servant's heart. It has been estimated that 40 per cent of the people who seek professional counselling first go to a pastor for help. Leaders are in the people business and the shepherding paradigm best reflects that reality. As Marshall points out, '[Leaders] are always talking with their people and they are always listening to their people . . . The good shepherd . . . *"calls his sheep by name"* (John 10:3 – my emphasis), that is, he knows their characteristics and their temperaments and their individual identities.'[332] The Christian leader, then, especially the pastor, but also including the missionary on the front lines of pioneer work, or in working in support roles vis-à-vis the national church, will have contextualized, in the sense of identifying with and understanding his people. This makes him or her all the more effective in shepherding the flock.

---

[332] Tom Marshall, *Understanding Leadership*, 22–3.

10

Stickability: Finishing well, like the Master

As we all know, it is one thing to start a race and another thing to finish it well. The Kenyan Olympian cross-country skier understood the importance of finishing well. So did the six-times winner of the ten thousand km event at the 1998 Winter Olympics in Japan, Norwegian Bjorn Dahlie. When Dahlie crossed the finishing line he did not rush off to a victory party. Instead, he waited patiently for the man who came in last in the 92-competitor field, Philip Boit of Kenya.

Boit had only begun skiing two years previously when he first laid eyes on snow! Now he had become the first African to qualify for this event. Philip actually did not cross the finishing line until half an hour after the victor had completed it. He was met there by Bjorn Dahlie himself who lifted Boit in a bear hug of congratulations, communicating his respect for the African's determination to finish.

The ultimate servant, the Lord Jesus Christ finished well too. The final mark of servanthood that *tys* leaders of all stripes together is stickability, the ability to persevere to the end of the race, of the job, yes, of life itself. It is much easier to start well than to finish well as a leader. Of Christ's embodiment of this principle of stickability, we read in Scripture a stirring exhortation.

Therefore, since we are surrounded by such a great cloud of witnesses, let us throw off everything that hinders and the sin that so easily entangles, and let us run with perseverance the race marked out for us. Let us fix our eyes on Jesus, the author and perfecter of our faith, who for the joy set before him endured the cross, scorning its shame, and sat down at the right hand of the throne of God. Consider him who endured such opposition from sinful men, so that you will not grow weary and lose heart. In your struggle against sin, you have not yet resisted to the point of shedding your blood.[333]

Even non-believers in pondering the patterns of effective leadership acknowledge the essentiality of perseverance in leaders. A five-year study of 90 excellent leaders and their followers led to the identifying of four common areas of competence shared by all 90 leaders. We particularly draw your attention to the third trait – which really is another way of defining perseverance.

1. *Management of attention:* The ability to communicate a sense of outcome, goal, or direction that attracts followers. We might call this vision.
2. *Management of meaning:* The ability to create and communicate meaning with clarity and understanding. We might call this communication skills.
3. *Management of trust:* The ability to be reliable and consistent so people can count on them. We might call this perseverance.
4. *Management of self:* The ability to know one's self and to use one's skills within limits of strengths and weaknesses. We might call this self-discipline.[334]

---

[333] Hebrews 12:1–5.
[334] Warren Bennis cited in Paul Hershey and Kenneth Blanchard, *Management of Organizational Behavior*, 98.

The high incidence of leaders not finishing well

Finishing well is described by Bobby Clinton, whom we have referred to earlier as being an expert on the study of Christian leadership, as *convergence*. He bemoans the findings of his study of hundreds of Christian leaders – in the Bible and in church history – many of whom he feels did not achieve that final pinnacle of successful leadership for which God had been preparing them their whole lives. We all know leaders who have been toppled from high profile ministries by the magnetic pull of money, sex, or power. In addition to being leaders who have overcome the conflicts found in ministry – either from within or without – Clinton sees the leader who finishes well as being the one who is 'productive over a lifetime [through] a dynamic ministry philosophy that evolves continually from the interplay of three factors: biblical dynamics, personal gifts, and situational dynamics'.[335]

We looked at the issue of finishing well or not finishing well in the chapter on teachability as we thought about how the Lord shapes us redemptively both through our mistakes or by the power he gives us to obey from the outset, so we do not need to dwell on this aspect of leadership in depth here. Nonetheless it is only fitting to end this book by reflecting on our track record as leaders with a certain objectivity. Do we fit into the category of those like King Manasseh who ended his life on a positive note after decades of failure, failure that included murder, witchcraft, and sacrificing of children to the pagan deity Molech (2 Ki. 21; 2 Chron. 33)? Or are we in the group like King Solomon who started with a flash of brilliance but whose heart was led astray by promiscuity (1 Ki. 11:1–6), and hence who did not finish well as a leader?

---

[335] Bobby Clinton, *The Making of a Leader*, 180.

Wherever we are found on the continuum of faithfulness, it is never too late to change and make a fresh start (Lam. 3:22–23; 1 John 1:9). 'Whether forgiveness and second chances are graciously extended to us by the Lord as we move along in our leadership pilgrimmage, we can be sure that God works with the raw material of our lives and of how he has equipped us, and then gives us opportunities and tests in order to prepare us for the next step in being useful in his service.'[336] In this final chapter, then, we shall look at just a few of the practical tests that make or break a servant leader over the long haul. Most of them we have already reflected on in one way or another. These include a capacity to bear pain, an unrelenting commitment to self-discipline, and patience to wait for God's breakthrough.

Pain-bearing

In our honest moments, at times when we get together, Joseph D'Souza and I reminisce about how far God has taken us from the days we spent on the same evangelism team in India close to thirty years ago. Joseph says almost enviously that he wished he could do what I do, settle down, pastor a church, and put his good mind to work writing books! I know where he is coming from. He now virtually lives on an airplane flitting between east and west in his major leadership role in missions. His time is not his own when he is on the ground. Instead of being able to devote his time to his family or actual church planting in his own beloved country, he has to devote huge chunks of time to fund-raising so others can do

---

[336] 'The lesson of Karla Faye Tucker', *Christianity Today* (April, 1998), 15–16.

it! He endures death threats against himself. His dog was recently poisoned by someone who penetrated his home compound and about whom Joseph said, 'Certain people were trying to send me a message.' When I think of him and so many others I have been privileged to work with over the years in missions, the words of Paul come to mind in his description of the Christian life: 'For your [Christ's] sake we face death all day long; we are considered as sheep to be slaughtered' (Rom. 8:36).

Ministry is spiritual warfare and its leaders are special targets of the Evil One. We cannot get around it. Leaders can experience a lack of appreciation. They can be ambushed by the very people they have given themselves to sacrificially. They can be misunderstood when their intentions are honourable. These attacks take their toll over time. In fact, anyone who lives a godly life in Christ Jesus will suffer persecution (2 Tim. 3:12). That certainty of pain as a function of faithfulness (as well as joy; see the book of Philippians to notice the correlation) is captured ever so poignantly in *The Pilgrim's Progress*. As Christian makes his pilgrimage to heaven we see him beset on every side by temptations and Satanic assault. Take his descent into the Valley of Humiliation, for instance. There he is confronted by that 'foul fiend', Apollyon, who all but overcomes Christian who has already been wearied along the way. Not yet having faced Apollyon in battle, Christian, along with his companions Discretion, Piety, Charity, and Prudence, wonder what lies ahead. Discerningly, Christian remarks: 'As it was difficult coming up, so so far as I can see) it is dangerous going down.' 'Yes', replies Prudence, 'so it is, for it is a hard matter for a man to go down into the Valley of Humiliation, as thou art now, and to catch no slip by the way.'[337]

---

[337] John Bunyan, *The Pilgrim's Progress* (New York: Grosset & Dunlap Publishers, [*sic.*]), 69.

These people were 'watching and praying'. That is, they had an accurate understanding of the Christian life, one that is marked, as Romans 6–8 delineate, if read together as a unit and not sequentially, a life characterized by a mixture of struggle and success, of obstacles and overcoming.

As we have stressed in Chapter Five, there are ways to maintain our resilience as leaders in the face of the steady erosion of our morale, our confidence, or our faith. A daily tour of duty in the inner world enables us to ward off the dragons that might otherwise blow us away with their fiery breath. As we focus on the cross and that we are to follow in the footsteps of our Master who stood firm against all odds, we are able to embrace the pain that comes with leadership and not walk away, as so many seem to be doing these days. To endure the pain for a season enables us to escape the fate that Gordon MacDonald memorably alluded to in his talks to those of us gathered at the OM International Leaders Meetings in August, 1989 in De Bron, Holland, when he wryly observed: 'Some of us have discerned that the grass is greener on the other side of the fence – but so is the water bill!'

Gary Corwin, SIM (Sudan Interior Mission) missionary and until recently editor of the well-respected *Evangelical Missions Quarterly*, offers a sample of how persevering leaders endure pain in one of his editorials in that journal.

- They suffer from fatigue due to overwork.
- They are overwhelmed by an avalanche of conflicting duties and differing expectations from different stake-holders in the ministry.
- They often have to be the 'bad guy', that is, be the bearer of bad news or imposers of discipline.
- They have to hand-hold the self-centred in their midst.

- They have to make the hard decisions alone in times of crisis.
- They have to bear the pain of others.[338]

If that is not enough to scare you off leadership, fine, but then do that kind of leading for 40 years, and I'll not only take my hat off to you but I'll let you mentor me! Such stickability does not grow on trees and distinguishes the servant leader from the self-aggrandizing leader.

A sure sign of the disease of perseverance faltering is pessimism or cynicism in the leader. This is a disease of leadership more common in older than younger leaders. The older leader has had his or her fair share of disappointments and failures. This attitude can infect a whole congregation or organization. It is what Hebrews 12:15 calls a 'bitter root' by which many become defiled. Not to ruthlessly deal with this habit of mind and of speech is to *not* finish well. As one minister has put it, 'A minister may well become weary in body and faint at heart, as at times everyone does. But the truth is that people have enough troubles and burdens of their own without having to endure a pessimistic, critical pastor.'[339]

Some of this pain-bearing that comes from persevering is associated with what we talked about earlier, accessibility to those who work for you. Quite remarkably, historians note, George Washington was 'in the field' for virtually the entire eight year duration of the American Revolution. During one stretch, he did not return home to Virginia for six straight years. Moreover, after American independence, he, the first American president, spent almost twenty of the

---

[338] Gary Corwin, 'Leadership as Pain-Bearing', *Evangelical Missions Quarterly* (January 1998), 17.

[339] Bert B. Beach, 'Pitfalls of Ministry', *Ministry* (January 2001), 19.

next 45 years of his life away from his beloved Mount Vernon in the service of his country.[340] He often needed only several hours of sleep a night and was reputed to stay on horseback for several days at a time during crucial events of the Revolution when he needed to be on duty constantly. Washington was willing to endure the hardship imposed on him as a leader because he knew how important it was to circulate with his troops to boost morale, or to visit outlying areas of the country as a politician to impart his vision and to show he was not above mixing with the common man. Similarly, another American president, one with a physical disablement, Franklin Roosevelt, kept a crowded schedule of meetings and personal appointments while in the White House, even though confined to a wheel-chair.[341]

My wife and I, on our last visit to the United Kingdom, visited the cabinet war rooms where Winston Churchill and his key leaders bunkered down during the crucial years of World War Two. The crowded and spartan living conditions of the 21 underground rooms near Westminister in London revealed how much these people were prepared to sacrifice to get the job done. They endured short-term pain to get the long-term gain – which we alluded to in an earlier chapter as being a specific attribute of servant leadership.

One cannot help thinking too of pioneer missionaries who endured hardship to blaze a trail for the gospel in new territory under impossible conditions. The remoteness of their location and urgency of their ground-breaking work kept men like C.T. Studd and David Livingstone away

---

[340] Donald T. Phillips, *The Founding Fathers on Leadership: Classic Teamwork in Changing Times* (New York: Warner Books, 1997), 95.

[341] Ibid., 94.

from family and home for decades at a time. William
Carey laboured in a hardship-filled missionary career in
India spanning almost half a century. He buried the first
two of his three wives on the field. When asked what
quality best to find in a missionary recruit, he exclaimed,
'Give me plodders'. Amy Carmichael, also of India,
springs to mind as being another British missionary who,
once on the field, never looked back to the comforts of
home, identifying permanently with her new home. All
of these saints who have gone before us had this inde-
fatigable capacity for being pain-bearers, and thus were
able to persevere through thick and thin.

I close this section on pain-bearing in ministry as a key
to perseverance by sharing haunting e-mail diary notes I
lately received from a missionary friend of mine. This
e-mail chronicles one-week-in-the-life-of-a-missionary. To
protect the location of this missionary, ministering cross-
culturally with a gospel-resistant people, I have disguised
some details. What struck me as I read these anguished
reflections was how wearing it is to live in this part of the
world. This missionary family ministers out of a context
of pain and struggle. I only share you one day's journal.
All seven are filled with disappointments, spiritual
oppression, danger, and uncertainties. To think that this
family has been in this part of the world for decades
under such circumstances only illustrates vividly what I
mean by bearing one's cross daily and unfalteringly as
the key to advancing the kingdom of God.

*'Thursday afternoon Lynne and I had just sat down for an
afternoon coffee, when we noticed that Nathaniel, one of our
national staff in our media work, was mysteriously walking by
our house. What was he doing here? Although he and others
come over regularly for work, we always notify each other.
Today he appeared extremely tense. What had gone wrong this*

time? He breathed nervously as he related his story. He and another national staff member had been apprehended by the police that afternoon. Police regularly apprehend these people who are in the minority in the population, hassle them, and threaten them in order to get bribes from them. The police took their passports, which had valid visas, and threatened to send both men back to their homeland unless they paid him a steep bribe. They gave him the equivalent of three days of police pay. The policeman was apparently about to let them go when two other officers showed up, who in turn wanted their share of the bribe. As they all walked toward the police station, these nationals feared that once they were inside the police station they could be beaten and tortured and who knows when they would ever get out. So, on the pretext of having to prepare for upcoming religious rituals, they escaped. Jumping into a taxi, Nathaniel soon arrived at our house, never having been so frightened in his life. Though Nathaniel had escaped, the passports were with the police now. While it is easy for a national to get a new passport from his embassy, Nathaniel feared that if their passports were in the police station, the police could easily trump up a case against them. Somehow we had to retrieve those passports. We found Matthew, who had escaped to Nathaniel's home, and the three of us drove to the police station to see if I could complain to the supervisor. It was close to closing time for the shift and so no higher officer was on duty. I decided to ask the pastor of the local church for advice. He warned me that I might be implicated if I got involved, but suggested a certain police superintendent who had served them well a year ago when the church had some legal problems. It was late by then, so the next day I drove to the police station wondering what I would face there. Regardless of possible negative repercussions, I knew I had to exercise solidarity with our national colleagues. The official was very polite and did not ask one question as to my relationship with these two men. He sent his assistant to check into the matter. He came back *and said there was no information of any passports being confiscated. The superintendent told me that without the name of the policeman there was nothing they could do. Fortunately Matthew had noticed the badge number on his belt and remembered it. I said to the officer, "Does # 1446 make any sense?" And so the assistant was sent to find # 1446. I waited and waited in the police station praying and wondering if this was just a waste of time. An hour later the assistant returned, and sure enough, both passports were in his hands! I couldn't believe it! He gave me them, but then the superintendent stepped in and said, "We can't give these passports to you; these men have to come here themselves." And so I was on the road again. I picked up Nathaniel (Matthew was not in his house) and returned to the station. By now it was noon hour and so we waited nearly two hours before the assistant returned from lunch. He smiled quietly as he pulled out Nathaniel's passport and then also the money he had taken from him the day before. Nathaniel signed that he had received the passport and the money, and then as we stepped outside the station, the policeman in question was there, and sheepishly offered his apologies to Nathaniel. The next day we were able to collect Matthew's passport without further waiting or deliberate delays by the police. The entire ordeal cost me at least 12 hours of work time plus over 100 km of travel, but at least we were able to retrieve the passports.'*

A total commitment to a lifestyle of discipline

As we think of pain-bearing as a lifestyle in order to become a servant leader with excellence, I think of the importance of possessing a willingness to seize the small moments in order to be all the more productive. George Verwer listens to tapes while he is jogging. I keep a book or magazine in a half dozen places so that I can use days filled with the odd moment of 'down time' productively to learn. This self-discipline is rarely acquired suddenly, but it does separate the good leader from the also-rans. One thinks of educator's Horace Mann's dictate: 'Habits are like a cable. We weave a strand of it everyday and soon it cannot be broken.' When interviewed while serving as US Secretary of State in the ill-fated final months of the Nixon administration, Alexander Haig made a telling statement in opining about what separates the men from the boys in leadership: 'Vision without discipline is a daydream.'

Another of the founding fathers of the modern American state was exemplary in demonstrating this self-discipline which as a way of life enables one to persevere. I refer to John Adams, who was a lawyer and yet who never felt that he had arrived intellectually, proving to be a lifelong avid reader who determined never to 'suffer one hour unimproved'.[342] Harry Truman, American president following the Second World War, perceptively observed that 'not all readers can be leaders. But all leaders must be readers.'[343]

Now the thing of it is that leaders just do not have much time for sitting down by the fireplace with a good book in hand. We are talking here about developing habits of endurance whereby the little moments are seized – as well as larger chunks of time purposefully set aside for reflective learning even though to do so puts pressure on other aspects of one's schedule. We've already addressed this discipline of reading in the chapter on maintaining personal vitality so I do not want to belabour the point. The main thing I want to emphasize here is how imperative it is to intentionalize effective and efficient use of time. It is to take seriously the injunction of Ephesians to

[342] Ibid., 32.
[343] Ibid., 169.

be 'making the most of every opportunity, because the days are evil' (5:16). Such self-discipline results in a way of life like John Wesley who in his journals speaks of dividing his waking hours up into five minute segments.

I realize how frequently I have drawn on the life of Wesley to illuminate several servant leadership principles. I cannot therefore fail to include his counterpart in being a giant evangelist of the eighteenth century in Great Britain, George Whitefield, at least once in this book. I do so now because, paradoxically, even though Welsey was the luminary who was reputed to be so methodical and self-disciplined, Whitefield, on the other hand, being cast as spontaneous and charismatic, was a giant of the faith every bit as disciplined as Wesley, let alone one with whom I feel more compatibility doctrinally. About his self-discipline these words are penned by one of his biographers: 'While many a student [speaking of his university days] wasted his days in frivolity, Whitefield practiced the Holy Club's severe discipline, planning each hour and forcing himself to do as he planned, "that no moment be lost." His personality became cast in this mold of self-mastery, and in our study of his life a recognition of these habits will help us to understand the otherwise inexplicable immensity of his accomplishments.'[344] Indeed, although it is the Spirit-filled person whom God uses the most, it is also true that leaders who shine the brightest are also very self-disciplined people. After all, 'self-control' is listed as one of the fruits of the Spirit (Gal. 5:23).

Thomas Edison, the inventor of the light bulb and many other electrical devices, defined genius as '1% inspiration

---

[344] Arnold A. Dallimore, *George Whitefield: God's Anointed Servant in the Great Revival of the Eighteenth Century* (Westchester, IL: Crossway Books, 1990), 16.

and 99% perspiration'.[345] To succeed in your endeavours,
you must plan to succeed: that is why I take the first 15
minutes of most work days to plan out my whole day. I
also map out my schedule a week at a time and six weeks
at a time and a year at a time. Periodically those plans
have to be adjusted and recalibrated to keep in step with
the Holy Spirit (Eph. 5:25). But planning carefully
enables me, for example, to slot in six hours a week (an
hour here, an hour there) to devote myself to writing.
Similarly I pencil in preparation time for post-graduate
courses that I teach on the side as a seminary adjunct
faculty member. Moreover, I plan 'dates' with my wife,
phone calls to our son, thrice weekly times for jogging,
and so forth. Of course, you not only need a plan to work
but you need to work the plan. Some people delude
themselves into thinking that theorizing about self-
discipline is the same as self-discipline. You need both:
the dream and the diligence. Then you will not be overwhelmed by the unexpected. That structure allows you
to be flexible paradoxically whereas the person living on
the edge of chaos because of an undisciplined life easily
gets stressed by the unexpected: there is no more emotional room for pressure. You will have developed the
spiritual backbone to run the course, to be a perseverer as
a leader. Or, as Romans 12:11 puts it, you will have
proven that you are never 'lacking in zeal, but keep your
spiritual fervour, serving the Lord' (cf. 2 Thess. 3:13; Prov.
22:29; 1 Pet. 1:13; 2 Tim. 2:15).

---

[345] John Stott, *Issues Facing Christians Today*, 331.

Patience in the eye of the storm

One of the chief reasons why leaders do not attain stickability, and so forfeit their right to be called servant leaders, is that they have not remained centred in God. A failure to draw on the Source of power that is higher than we are explains why those who move beyond dreaming to doing with self-discipline nevertheless can falter (fail to persevere) when the trials and tribulations of life set in. The technological advances of our age have reduced our capacity to be patient. E-mails for instance enable us to respond instantaneously to communications by those separated from us geographically, whereas our forefathers, especially where oceans were involved, might wait six months or more for a response to a letter. Patience is essential in the Christian life. Instant results are rare in either conversion or sanctification (James 5:8). I have been struck in preaching through the book of Revelation in my church at the time of writing about how frequently perseverance is associated with overcoming in the churches (e.g. Rev. 1:9; 2:2,3,10,13,19,26; 3:8,10,21). A Christian leader visiting an American Christian college library keyed in the word 'success' in their computer data base and got 217 hits. He then keyed in the word 'faithfulness' and got no hits! With the will to persevere in short supply in our culture and in our churches, we should not be surprised, then, to find it all too absent in a good many of our leaders. Just as parishioners deal with problems by running away from them, shifting churches, so pastors or Christian leaders frequently deal with hardship in the ministry by running away from their problems, skipping to another church or another field or another organization – instead of facing the music, instead of persevering.

This quality of perseverance is reflected well in an encounter with Sisters of Charity workers Philip Yancey

describes having visited in Calcutta.[346] I can well imagine
the conditions of filth, disease, and poverty they would
have worked in, having visited Calcutta myself. There,
these nuns minister to the poorest-of-the-poor without
making any evident dent in the sheer numbers of those
without hope in this life. But what gripped Yancey was
the tranquillity of the nuns. He traces that serenity back
to the rhythm of their day, which begins at 4:00 a.m. with
chapel, where, in their white saris, they pray and sing,
centring themselves in the love of God. Some years ago,
in spite of the pressure of constant demands, Mother
Teresa instituted a rule that requires these nuns to take
Thursdays off for prayer and rest. Additionally, they
begin their day with God and end it with God and so
develop the calmness (read patience) to persevere in
impossible conditions.

In listing a set of characteristics that distinguish the
servant leader from an ordinary leader, George Mallone
has said much the same thing in contending that
'servants know their ultimate reward for service is found
in their relationship with the Lord'. He goes on to say
that 'servants often are discouraged and frustrated, yet
they remember that their reward is from God and with
that they are content'.[347] In prefiguring the Servant of the
Lord, the Messiah, Isaiah 49:4 captures this patience in
the midst of suffering cultivated out of a deep relationship with the living God with these words: 'But I said,
"I have laboured to no purpose; I have spent my strength
in vain and for nothing. Yet what is due me is in the
LORD's hand, and my reward is with my God."'
Patience emanating from a close walk with God enables

---

[346] Philip Yancey, *Reaching for the Invisible God* (Grand Rapids,
MI: Zondervan, 2000), 83.
[347] George Mallone, *Furnace of Renewal*, 88.

one to persevere and therefore be able to avoid disappointing the ones who watch us closely for inspiration and leadership. Perseverance is an indispensable aspect of servant leadership.

Perseverance waits for God's timing to vindicate. To give growth. To justify all that time and energy invested in others. It is surely what is in mind when Paul writes in Galatians 6:9: 'Let us not become weary in doing good, for at the proper time [*kairos* in the Greek] we will reap a harvest if we do not give up.' Note the perseverance enjoined at the end of the verse, and at the beginning, and that is fuelled by a childlike trust in God's sovereignty and benevolence as it relates to our work for him. Nor should it go unnoticed that, in the context, Paul is encouraging those who are doing little acts of kindness or good works (vv. 6–8) to continue to engage in them because God will reward such a labour of love if those deeds are persevered in. A testimony to the truthfulness of this promise is the ministry of Arab World Ministries in North Africa. After one hundred years of existence, this mission, until 1985 known as North Africa Mission, had seen perhaps five indigenous churches established in the five Maghreb countries of Mauritania, Morocco, Algeria, Tunisia, and Libya. Today, some twenty years later, it is estimated by those knowledgeable about the area, that there are at least a hundred national churches in North Africa. There has been a people movement especially among the Kabyles in Algeria, spearheaded by nationals, which has caught the evangelical world pleasantly by surprise and given testimony once again to a God who is the God of the breakthrough. A true servant leader rises to the occasion, digging in heels in the face of adversity, remembering the example of the Master who did not even have a place to lay his head down in comfort at night as he proclaimed day-by-day the

kingdom of heaven throughout Palestine. John Stott has it
right, then, when he explains the importance of perseverance in leadership as follows: 'The real leader . . . has
the resilience to take setbacks in his stride, the tenacity to
overcome fatigue and discouragement . . . The real leader
adds to vision and industry the grace of perseverance.'[348]

Many of us have been aided in our inner journey by
Oswald Chamber's *My Utmost for His Highest*. One of
the recurring themes in his devotionals is the need to
'let go and let God'. Thus we find him artfully penning
these words about the need for patience in waiting
for the breakthrough in ministry, in these words:
'Every vision [from God] will be made real if we
will have patience. Think of the enormous leisure of God!
He is never in a hurry. We are always in such a frantic
hurry . . . God has to take us into the valley, and put
us through fires and floods to batter us into shape, until
we get to the place where He can trust us with the
veritable reality.'[349]

Conclusion

One more thought about the patience to wait for a
breakthrough. It relates to a sense of calling to what we
do. Leaders lead because God gives them a vision for a
particular kingdom-enlarging task or to work with a
certain group of people for the same reason. That calling
may change from time to time. I have moved from being
a front-line missionary to a behind-the-scenes missionary
to a missions' executive pastor to a missionary educator

---

[348] John Stott, *Issues Facing Christians Today*, 333.
[349] Oswald Chambers, *My Utmost for His Highest*, (New York:
Dodd, Mead & Company, 1935), 188.

to a pastor to a theological educator of pastors. Never have I moved before I sensed I was called to move on. Never have I moved on because I folded to the pressure of a negative situation, instead getting out while the going was good. I admire ice hockey legend Wayne Gretsky because he retired in his late thirties while he was still an all-star performer. We have all seen in various professional sports those who stayed on to play the game long after their skills had eroded to a pale imitation of their former glory. Therefore I agree with H.B. London, pastor to pastors, when he exhorts: 'Pastors must commit to stay in an assignment until God gives them a genuine spiritual breakthrough or a clear-cut release.'[350] I suspect that far too many works of God are stillborn because leaders have bailed out too soon and thus hindered what God wanted to do.

---

[350] H.B. London and N.B. Wiseman, *The Heart of a Great Pastor*, 27.

Conclusion

If you will recall my musings in the introduction, as a young leader, I was befuddled about how servanthood squared with leadership. The two did not seem to mix – at least with my personality and natural ability to lead. Along the way, I trust you sense that the paradox of servant leadership has been clarified for me. The reconciliation of the two ideas is well expressed by the authors of *Leadership by the Book* and so I will let them express what I have groped toward saying throughout this book.

> I believe there are two kinds of leaders: those who are *leaders first* and those who are *servants first* ... People who are leaders first are often those who naturally try to control, to make decisions, to give orders. They're 'driven' to lead – they want to be in charge. And they're possessive about their leadership position – they think they own it. They don't like feedback because they see it as threatening their position, the one thing they most want to hold on to ...
>
> Leaders who are *servants first* will assume leadership only if they see it as the best way they can serve. They're 'called' to lead, rather than driven, because they naturally want to be helpful. They aren't possessive about their leadership position – they view it as an act of stewardship rather than

ownership. If someone else on the scene is a better leader, they're willing to partner with that person or even step aside to find another role for themselves where they can better serve.[351]

By God's grace, over the years, I guess I would have to admit that I have been a slow learner of servant leadership but now I would like to think that I am what these gentlemen are talking about above – a servant first and a leader second. After seeing a TV mini-series on Franklin D. Roosevelt and his role in the Second World War last summer, I can well imagine the following exchange that took place concerning the motive of Roosevelt's ever-present right-hand man, Harry Hopkins. Apparently, once, when Wendell Wilkie, a key government leader, was visiting Franklin Roosevelt, he saw Harry Hopkins at Roosevelt's side. Wilkie's reaction was: 'Mr President, why do you keep that frail, sickly man, Harry Hopkins, at your elbow?' Roosevelt replied, 'Through that door flows daily an incessant stream of men and women who almost invariably want something from me. Harry Hopkins wants only to serve me.' Can we too honestly say that our only motive in leadership is to serve the Lord Jesus Christ and his people? If we can say 'yes' to that query, then we are what Scripture calls a *servant leader*.

We who are leaders or aspiring leaders, or future leaders, even if we do not realize it yet, must not quickly give up on ourselves. Christ has set a high standard and yet he says to the faltering servant leader, 'Come to me, all you who are weary and burdened, and I will give you rest. Take my yoke upon you and learn from me, for I am

[351] Kenneth Blanchard, Bill Hybels, and Phil Hodges, *Leadership by the Book: Tools to Transform Your Workplace* (New York: WaterBrook Press, 1999), 42.

gentle and humble in heart, and you will find rest for your souls. For my yoke is easy and my burden is light' (Matt. 11:28–30).

Most Christians, as far as I can tell, are slow learners about servant leadership. Let us be then like John Stephen Akhwari of Tanzania, who represented his country in the 1968 marathon. Along the way in this final event of the Olympics, he fell hard and injured both his ankle and his knee. Undeterred, he got his leg wrapped in a bandage that soon became bloody. Nevertheless, he continued the race. Long after an Ethiopian had won, limping into the entrance of the stadium to run the final lap of the 26 mile race, Akhwari completed the race. Asked later by a reporter why he had bothered to finish a race he could neither win nor finish well in, the Tanzanian said: 'My country did not send me seven thousand miles to begin a race; they sent me to finish the race.' Even so may our own attitude be as we seek to become the leader who is paramountly a servant of others.

Bibliography

Anderson, Leith, *Dying For Change* (Minneapolis, MN: Bethany House Publishers, 1990)

Bass, Dorothy C., 'Rediscovering The Sabbath', *Christianity Today* (September 1, 1997), 39–43

Beach, Bert B., 'Pitfalls of Ministry', *Ministry* (January 2001), 18–19

Beck, John D. and Neil M. Yeager, *The Leader's Window: Mastering the Four Styles of Leadership to Build High-Performing Teams* (New York: John Wiley and Sons Inc., 1994)

Bennis, Warren and Burt Nanus, *Leaders: The Strategies for Taking Charge* (New York: Harper & Row, 1985)

Blanchard, Kenneth H., 'Listening: A Basic Business Survival Skill', *Insider Guide* (June/July 1992), 12, 18

_____ , Bill Hybels, and Philip Hodges, *Leadership by the Book: Tools to Transform Your Workplace* (New York: WaterBrook Press, 1999)

Bonhoeffer, Dietrich, *Life Together* (New York: Harper & Row, 1954)

Bonk, Jonathan J., *Missions and Money: Affluence as a Western Missionary Problem* (Maryknoll, NY: Orbis Books, 1991)

Brouwer, Paul J., 'The Power to See Ourselves', *Harvard Business Review* (November/December 1964), 36–43

Brown, Peter, *Augustine of Hippo* (Berkeley, CA: University of California Press, 1967)

Bunyan, John, *The Pilgrim's Progress* (New York: Grosset & Dunlap Publishers, [*sic.*])

Burns, James M., *Leadership* (New York: Harper & Row, 1978)

Callaghan, Kenon L., *Effective Church Leadership: Building on the Twelve Keys* (New York: HarperSan Francisco, 1990)

Chambers, Oswald, *My Utmost for His Highest* (New York: Dodd, Mead & Company, 1935)

Chandapilla, P.T., *Jesus The Master Trainer* (Bombay: Gospel Literature Service, 1985)

Chatterjee, Sunil, 'Memories of Serampore Translations', *Dharma Deepika* (June 1999), 59–66

Clinton, Bobby, *The Making of a Leader* (Colorado Springs, CO: NavPress, 1988)

Corwin, Gary, 'Leadership as Pain-Bearing', *Evangelical Missions Quarterly* (January 1998), 17

Covey, Stephen, *First Things First* (New York: Fireside, 1994)

_____ , *Principle-Centered Leadership* (New York: Fireside, 1991)

_____ , *The 7 Habits of Highly Effective People* (New York: Simon & Schuster, Inc., 1990)

Dallimore, Arnold A., *George Whitefield: God's Anointed Servant of the Eighteenth Century* (Westchester, IL: Crossway Books, 1990)

_____ , *Spurgeon* (Edinburgh: The Banner of Truth Trust, 1995)

Dayton, Ed, 'Modelling', *Christian Leadership Letter* (published in Monrovia, CA: World Vision International, July 1978)

Deal, Torrance and A. Kennedy, *Corporate Cultures* (Reading, MA: Addison-Wesley, 1989)

DePree, Max, *Leadership Is an Art* (East Lansing, MI: Michigan State University Press, 1987)

_____ , 'Leadership Jazz', in J. Thomas Wren (ed.), *The Leader's Companion: Insight on Leadership Through the Ages* (New York: The Free Press, 1995)

DeSilva, Ranjit, 'The Missing Ingredient in Leadership Training', *Evangelical Missions Quarterly* (January 1996), 50–6.

Deutschman, Alan, 'The CEO's Secret of Managing Time', *Fortune* (June 1, 1992), 135–146

Downing, Jim, *Meditation* (Colorado Springs, CO: NavPress, 1976)

Drucker, Peter F., 'Managing Oneself', *Harvard Business Review* (March/April 1999), 65–74

_____ , *The Effective Executive* (New York: HarperCollins, 1985)

_____ , 'Your Leadership Is Unique', *Leadership* (Fall 1996), 54–5

Ecker, Richard E., *Staying Well: Why the Good Life Is Bad for Your Health* (Downer's Grove, IL: InterVarsity Press, 1984)

The Economist, 'Ready, Fire, Aim' (December 6, 1997), 74

Edwards, Judson, 'Turn It the Other Way', *Leadership* (Summer 1999), 40–4

Edwards, Rex D., 'Service Over Self-Interest', *Ministry* (November 1997), 17–19

Engstrom, Ted, *The Fine Art of Mentoring* (Brentwood, TN: Wolgemuth & Hyatt, 1989)

_____ , *The Making of a Christian Leader* (Grand Rapids, MI: Zondervan, 1976)

Escobar, Samuel, 'The Internationalization of Missions and Leadership Style' (speech given to EFMA annual conference in 1991)

Finnie, Kellsye M., *William Carey: By Trade A Cobbler* (Eastbourne, UK: Kingsway Publications, 1986)

Finzel, Hans, *The Top Ten Mistakes Leaders Make* (Wheaton, IL: Victor Books, 1994)

Fischer, Louis, *Gandhi: His Life and Message for the World* (New York: Mentor Books, 1960)

Forbes, Cheryl, *The Religion of Power* (Bromley, England: MARC, 1986)

Ford, Leighton, *Transforming Leadership* (Downer's Grove, IL: InterVarsity Press, 1991)

Foster, Richard, *Celebration of Discipline* (Sevenoaks, UK: Hodder & Stoughton, 1984)

_____ , *The Challenge of the Disciplined Life* (San Francisco: HarperCollins Publishers, 1998)

Gangel, Kenneth O., *Feeding & Leading: A Practical Handbook on Administration in Churches and Christian Organizations* (Grand Rapids, MI: Baker Books, 1989)

Gardener, John, *On Leadership* (New York: The Free Press, 1993)

George, Timothy, *Faithful Witness: The Life and Mission of William Carey* (Birmingham, AB: New Hope, 1991)

Graham, Carol, *Azariah of Dornakal* (Madras, India: Christian Literature Service – revised edition 1972)

Green, Michael, *Freed to Serve* (Sevenoaks, UK: Hodder & Stoughton, 1983)

Greenleaf, Robert K., *The Power of Servant Leadership*, Larry C. Spears (ed.), (San Francisco: Berrett-Koehler, 1998)

Hammond, John S., Ralph L. Keeney, and Howard Raiffa, 'The Hidden Traps in Decision Making', *Harvard Business Review* (September/October 1998), 47–58

Hershey, Paul and Kenneth H. Blanchard, *Management of Organizational Behavior: Utilizing Human Resources* (Englewood Cliffs, NJ: Prentice Hall, 1993, 6th edition)

Hiebert, Paul G., *Anthropological Insights for Missionaries* (Grand Rapids, MI: Baker Book House, 1994)

Hill, Linda and Suzy Wetlaufer, 'Leadership When There

Is No One to Ask: An Interview with ENI's Franco Bernabe', *Harvard Business Review* (July/August 1998), 81–94

Holmes, R. Leslie, 'Be Sure To Leave Your Light On!', *Ministry* (November 1998), 5–7

Howell, Don N., 'Confidence in the Spirit as the Governing Ethos of the Pauline Mission', in C. Douglas McConnell (ed.), *The Holy Spirit and Mission Dynamics* (Pasadena, CA: William Carey Library, 1997), 36–65

Ingleby, Jonathan, 'Trickling Down or Shaking the Foundations: Is Contextualization Neutral?', *Missiology: An International Review, V.* 25 (2), (April 1997), 183–7

Johnstone, Patrick, *Operation World* 5th ed. (Grand Rapids, MI: Zondervan, 1993)

Jones, Bruce W., *Ministerial Leadership in a Managerial World* (Wheaton, IL: Tyndale House, 1988)

Kanter, Rosabeth Moss, *The Change Masters: Innovation & Entrepreneurship in the American Corporation* (New York: Simon & Schuster, 1984)

Keyes, Larry and Larry Pate, 'Two-Thirds World Missions: The Next One Hundred Years', *Missiology: An International Review* 21(2) (April 1993), 187–206

Kirkpatrick, Shelly A., and Edwin A. Locke, 'Leadership: Do Traits Matter?' In J. Thomas Wren (ed.) *The Leader's Companion: Insights on Leadership Through the Ages* (New York: The Free Press, 1995), 133–143

Lindgren, Alvin J. and Norman Shawchuck, *Management for Your Church* (Nashville, TN: Abingdon, 1978)

Lao-tzu, 'Tao Te Ching,' In J. Thomas Wren (ed.), *The Leader's Companion: Insights On Leadership Through the Ages* (New York: The Free Press, 1995), 69–71

Longenecker, Harold L., *Growing Leaders by Design: How to Use Biblical Principles for Leadership Development* (Grand Rapids, MI: Kregel Resources, 1999)

London, H.B. and Neil B. Wiseman, *The Heart of a Great Pastor: How to Grow Strong and Thrive Wherever God Has Planted You* (Ventura, CA: Regal Books, 1994)

Lundy, J. David, *We Are the World: Globalisation and the Changing Face of Missions* (Carlisle, UK: OM Publishing, 1999)

_____, 'Moving Beyond Internationalizing the Missionary Force', *International Journal of Frontier Missions* 16(3) (Fall 1999), 147–155

Mallone, George, *Furnace of Renewal: A Vision for the Church* (Downer's Grove, IL: InterVarsity Press, 1981)

Marshall, Tom, *Understanding Leadership: Fresh Perspectives on the Essentials of New Testament Leadership* (Chichester, England: Sovereign World, 1991)

MacDonald, Gordon, 'Monday Morning Restoration', *Leadership* (Winter 1998), 28–32

_____, Gordon, *Ordering Your Private World* (Nashville, TN: Thomas Nelson Publishers, 1985)

_____, *Rebuilding Your Broken World* (Crowborough, UK: Highland Books, 1988)

McFarlane, Lynne J., Larry E. Senn, and John R. Childress, 'Redefining Leadership for the Next Century,' in J. Thomas Wren (ed.), *The Leader's Companion: Insight on Leadership through the Ages* (New York: The Free Press, 1995), 456–463

McGrath, Alister, *Christian Theology: An Introduction* (Oxford: Blackwell Publishers, 1994)

McGugan, Ian, 'The Five Worst Types Of Bosses', *Small Business* (November 1989), 42–45

McKenna, David, *Power To Follow, Grace To Lead* (Dallas, TX: Word, 1989)

Merton, Thomas, *The Last of the Fathers* (New York: Harcourt, Brace, and Company, 1954)

_____ , *Spiritual Direction and Meditation* (Collegeville, MN: The Liturgical Press, 1960)

Miller, Calvin, *Leadership: Thirteen Lessons for Individuals or Groups* (Colorado Springs, CO: NavPress, 1987)

Myers, Kenneth A., *All God's Children and Blue Suede Shoes: Christians and Popular Culture* (Westchester, IL: Crossway Books, 1989)

Naisbitt, John and Patricia Aburdene, *Reinventing The Corporation: Transforming Your Job and Your Company for the New Information Society* (New York: Warner, 1985)

Nanus, Burt, *Visionary Leadership* (San Francisco: Jossey-Bass, 1992)

Nee, Watchman, *The Normal Christian Worker* (Bombay: Gospel Literature Service, *sic*.)

Ortberg, John C., 'Taking Care of Busyness,' *Leadership* (Fall 1998), 28–34

Osei-Mensah, Gottfried, *Wanted: Servant Leaders* (Accra, Ghana: Africa Christian Press, 1990)

Packer, J.I., *Keeping in Step with the Spirit* (Grand Rapids, MI: Fleming Revell, 1994)

_____ , *A Quest for Godliness: The Puritan Vision of the Christian Life* (Wheaton, IL: Crossway Books, 1990)

Parshall, Phil, 'Why Some People Are Unproductive,' *Evangelical Missions Quarterly* (June 1990), 246–251

Peters, Thomas J. and Robert H. Waterman, *In Search of Excellence: Lessons from America's Best-Run Companies* (New York: Warner Books, 1982)

Peterson, Eugene, *The Contemplative Pastor* (Grand Rapids, MI: W.B. Eerdmans, 1993)

Phillips, Donald T., *The Founding Fathers on Leadership: Classic Teamwork in Changing Times* (New York: Warner Books, 1997)

Piper, John, *Let the Nations Be Glad: The Story of God in Missions* (Grand Rapids, MI: Baker Book House, 1996)

Pollard, William C., *The Soul of the Firm* (Grand Rapids, MI: Zondervan, 1996)

Quick, Thomas L., *Successful Team Building* (New York: AMACON, 1992)

Ratz, Calvin C., 'Satisfying People,' *Faith Today* (September/October 1992), 53

Richards, Larry, *A New Face for the Church* (Grand Rapids, MI: Zondervan, 1981)

_____, *A Practical Theology of Spirituality* (Grand Rapids, MI: Academie Books, 1987)

Rowe, Alan and Richard Mason, *Managing With Style: A Guide To Understanding, Assessing, and Improving Decision Making* (San Francisco: Jossey-Bass, 1989)

Ryken, Leland, *Work and Leisure in Christian Perspective* (Portland, OR: Multnomah Press, 1987)

Sanders, J. Oswald, *Spiritual Leadership* (Chicago: Moody Press, 1978)

Schmidt, Wayne, 'Sharing Goals and Life', *Leadership* (Summer 1999), 101

Senge, Peter, *The Fifth Dimension: The Art and Practice of the Learning Organization* (New York: Doubleday, 1990)

Sharp, Richard, 'Modelling It: If You Don't Model It, They Won't Do It!', *Frontline* (August/September 1992), 30–1

Shawcross, William, *Murdoch* (New York: Simon & Schuster, 1994)

Shepherd, Victor A., *So Great A Cloud of Witnesses* (Toronto: Light and Life Press Canada, 1993)

Sine, Thomas, *Mustard Seed Versus McWorld: Reinventing Life and Faith for the Future* (Grand Rapids, MI: Baker Book House, 1999)

Smith, Fred, 'Training To Reach the Top', *Leadership* (Spring 1996), 35–9

Snyder, Howard, *The Community of the King* (Downer's Grove, IL: InterVarsity Press, 1986)

_____, *The Radical Wesley and Patterns for Church Renewal* (Pasadena, CA: WIPF & Stock Publishers, 1996)

Sparks, Doug, 'Going Beyond Good Management', *Discipleship Journal* (Jan. 1982)

Stevens, R. Paul, *Liberating the Laity* (Downer's Grove, IL: InterVarsity Press, 1985)

Stewart, James A. *The Treasure House of Good Books* (Edinburgh: D. Mackay & Sons, 1969)

Stott, John, 'The Authority and Relevance of the Bible in the Modern World', *Crux* (June 1986), 17

_____, *The Cross of Christ* (Downer's Grove, IL: InterVarsity Press, 1986)

_____, *Issues Facing Christians Today* (Bombay: Gospel Literature Service, 1989)

_____, *The Preacher's Portrait* (Grand Rapids, MI: W.B. Eerdmans, 1972)

_____, 'What Makes Leadership Christian?' *Christianity Today* (August 9, 1985), 24–27

Thomas, Viv, *Future Leader* (Carlisle, UK: Paternoster Press, 1999)

Tillapaugh, Frank, *Unleashing the Church* (Ventura, CA: Regal Books, 1982)

Van Engel, Charles, *God's Missionary People: Rethinking the Purpose of the Local Church* (Grand Rapids, MI: Baker Book House, 1995)

Warren, Rick, *The Purpose Driven Church* (Grand Rapids, MI: Zondervan, 1995)

White, Charles E. 'What Wesley Practiced and Preached About Money', *Missions Frontiers Bulletin* (September/October 1994), 23–4

Willard, Dallas, *The Spirit of the Disciplines: Understanding How God Changes Lives* (San Francisco: HarperCollins, 1991)

Winzenburg, Stephen, 'Whatever Happened To Hospitality?', *Christianity Today* (May 22, 2000), 78–79

Yancey, Philip, *Reaching for the Invisible God* (Grand Rapids, MI: Zondervan, 2000)

Yu, Cecilia, ed., *A Winning Combination: Understanding the Cultural Tensions in Chinese Churches* (Petaluma, CA: Chinese Christian Mission, 1986)